OUT OF THE SHADOW: RESPONDING TO SUICIDE

Out of the Shadow

Responding to Suicide

76

Aidan Troy

VERITAS

First published 2009 by
Veritas Publications
7–8 Lower Abbey Street
Dublin 1
Ireland
Email publications@veritas.ie
Website www.veritas.ie

ISBN 978 1 84730 175 8

10 9 8 7 6 5 4 3 2 1

*A catalogue record for this book is available from the British
Library.*

Cover design by Lir Mac Cárthaigh
Printed in the Republic of Ireland by ColourBooks Ltd, Dublin

*Veritas books are printed on paper made from the wood pulp of
managed forests. For every tree felled, at least one tree is planted,
thereby renewing natural resources.*

For all those
who have come
out of the shadow
of suicide

Contents

Introduction

This book dealing with suicide is not one I ever thought I would write when I set out as a priest in 1971. As a student of theology in Dublin during the 1960s, the issue of suicide was summed up as a mortal sin as well as a crime. Indeed, prior to 23 April 2003, my awareness of suicide was limited to what I would read in newspapers and books. As a child growing up in Bray, Co. Wicklow, I vividly recall tiptoeing past a house where a person was said to have died by suicide. But all this was to change on that date in April 2003, when a 17-year-old took his life in Holy Cross Monastery garden, Belfast. This was the first time that suicide and its aftermath became part of my experience. I was profoundly affected and changed by witnessing the enormous sorrow and heartbreak of the family. This book is born out of that day and many others that were to follow.

Between Christmas Eve 2003 and St Valentine's Day 2004, fourteen young people from Protestant and Catholic communities in North and West Belfast died by suicide. Most were young males but there were females as well. While not all were in the parish where I was a priest at that time, some were.

On 14 February 2004, a young man hung himself from the top of Holy Cross bell tower. The church was undergoing restoration to mark its centenary and was covered with scaffolding. This 17-year-old had been at the funeral I had celebrated in Holy Cross church that morning for his friend who had hung himself in his family home a few days earlier. (Both these young people had been seriously injured in paramilitary punishment beatings the previous year.)

Suicides and the risk of suicide continued to be part of my life and ministry to many families and remains so even following my move from Belfast to another Passionist parish, St Joseph's in Paris, in September 2008. Families and individuals bereaved by suicide are all different and react in diverse ways. I hope to respect this and take this into account in this book. The sacred moments and confidences these families have shared with me following a suicide affect me still. The depth of their pain is beyond anything I could have imagined had these people not opened their hearts and homes to me. I feel privileged to have become part of their lives and remain in close contact with many of them to this day. I hope this book will be their gift to other individuals and families tempted to suicide or battling through the loss of a loved one following a suicide. While I take responsibility for what is contained in this book, the inspiration for it comes from the experience of individuals and families bereaved by suicides. In my estimation, they are among the bravest people I have met in my almost forty years of pastoral work.

This book does not claim to offer all the answers. It is not possible to neatly package the impact made by the discovery of one who has died or to plot out in detail the journey that lies ahead in the following days and years. This book offers some tentative suggestions and observations born of my experience, in the hope that they may be helpful in a pastoral context. There will be gaps that only readers can fill in the light of their own circumstances and outlooks. Some suggestions will be offered of resources that may be helpful, but they will be few. There are many statistics, medical opinions and sociological data that give background information and attempt to shed light on issues surrounding suicide. This book does not attempt to explain suicide as I believe it is not possible to do so.

I hope that this book will help a wide range of people who come into contact with suicide. Some will be the immediate family, neighbours and community. For others, it will be in the course of their particular work or calling. Among these will be medical and hospital personnel, ambulance and police services, suicide support groups and clergy, undertakers and morgue personnel. The circle can stretch even wider, when sometimes whole schools, colleges and parishes are involved. On many occasions, members of media organisations become involved in reporting a death by suicide. And there are those individuals, family member or near stranger, who unexpectedly encounter a suicide, maybe even by stumbling upon the body, or sense they are talking to someone seriously contemplating ending their life.

The first part of this book concentrates primarily on the pastoral needs of the family and surrounding community in the immediate aftermath of the death of a person by suicide. The time from the moment of discovery of death of the loved one to the funeral goodbye will be taken step by step, showing which elements seem to be particular to a death by suicide. I will also suggest what I have found helpful and point out some pitfalls that are best avoided.

The second part traces some of the challenges along the way in the first year after death and suggests some helpful pastoral responses. The emergence of suicide support and prevention groups in many places will be examined and some suggestions offered about how to start such a group where one is needed. Finally, the care of pastoral workers will be examined. These generous people also need support and help so they do not become exhausted and eventually ineffective in their reaching out.

While the book is written from the perspective of a Catholic priest, I hope it will offer support, encouragement and practical suggestions to people of all beliefs or none. It is offered to all involved in pastoral care whether they are ordained or not. Death is near us daily, in various forms, whether we have religious belief about the afterlife or not. But nothing has prepared us for the moment when it bursts into our own lives. We have never been there, even though we have heard about it since we were born. We know it will come to us but it is beyond our experience. In the meantime, we can, at best, search for greater understanding of it and ways to cope.

Even if the immediate family are believers, talk of God cannot always be assumed to be a good starting point when arriving into the aftermath of a suicide. God will never be absent from the situation, but can only be invoked for help or comfort if and when the bereaved indicate that they are ready. When people are lost in the midst of unbearable pain, struggling with loss beyond words, it may not be the best time for an outsider to bring God into the story. Reminding them of his presence may not bring the comfort intended by the person of faith. Indeed, God can be seen as the cause of their loss and pain. They may blame him and ask 'why?'

Following a suicide, there are added questions about why this happened and whether it could have been prevented. Suicide is utterly unique in that it goes contrary to the drive for life that characterises the human person. It is normal and understandable not to know how to respond to news of the suicide of a relative, friend, colleague, neighbour, classmate or other acquaintance. It is important not to feel that one should know precisely what to do or how to react.

Just after I was ordained a priest, I was offering a Mass of the Angels for a baby who had died on the eve of her baptism. The grief was tangible and I can still remember the numbness of the young couple that morning. In all the preparations for the funeral, the young mother had uttered not a word. Her feelings were beyond words. I did the best I could to deal with the situation sensitively, but I failed badly.

As I preached about the baby and God's part in the event of her death, the up-to-now silent young mother stood up in the front seat where she held the white coffin of her dead child. In an absolutely clear voice, she denounced me for daring to speak about her baby and God at the same time. 'How dare you,' she said, 'tell me what God was doing when my baby died.' She was totally right. I could feel the blood drain from my face and I knew that there was only one response: silence. It was necessary to let this young mother have her voice heard and appreciated. She was right and I was wrong. All I said was that I would continue with the Mass and remember what I had just heard.

Afterwards I met with that mother and she was able to tell me how devastated she was to hear the death of her beloved baby somehow caught up in the plan of God. I never forgot her words and to this day I remember with gratitude that young woman for teaching me a lesson that has stood me in good stead over the years. When I came face to face with so many suicides after 2003, I already had been formed and instructed by that mother thirty years before.

It is hoped that some pastoral skills will be developed by reading this book. But it must always be remembered that pastoral carers matter not for what they have done or will do, but because of who they are. When the pastoral worker enters the scene of a suicide or the danger of one, their best gift is their humanity shown through compassion, tenderness and love. That is all they have. That is everything and they need no more. The journey they begin with others, no matter how long or short it lasts, can resemble something of a wilderness. Pastoral companionship is not measured on a watch. It takes as long as it takes. As a pastoral carer the attitude has to remain that of an apprentice eager to learn.

PART I

Chapter 1

'I never thought this could come to my door'

Suicide is something we usually hear about in other families. Our hearts go out to those who are left heartbroken. We think (and hope) that it will never happen to us. But if the unimaginable happens and that person who so recently was part of us is gone, and gone by suicide, the world of meaning that we relied on is shattered. There is utter disbelief. This was not supposed to happen.

It is nearly impossible if you have not been there to describe what those first few moments following discovery are like. They are frightening to behold because you know that this person, this family, will never be the same again.

This chapter will deal with what a pastoral carer might find upon arrival at the scene of a suicide. The aim is to give some guidance on the role of the pastoral carer in these very early stages of the grieving process so soon after the suicide has been discovered. This chapter will also explore the different reactions people can have, including denial, anger, guilt and shame. Approaching and helping children who may have been close to the deceased must be done very delicately, especially if the child discovered the death. Some resources to help with this very sensitive matter will be indicated.

Being Present to the Pain

In those first few minutes after the discovery of the death, there is usually much activity as people move around without really knowing what to do. I believe that our body and mind protect us from the full horror of what has happened by allowing a kind of numbness to set in. Often I have seen people unable to think or to remember names and telephone numbers that at other times would be easily recalled.

There is no instruction book that can tell us how to cope with a suicide. It is in a category of its own. There is excellent research done on the topic in terms of gender, age and other factors. This research must continue in the struggle to understand and reduce the incidences of suicide. But at the moment of the discovery of the death of a loved one, information and statistics on suicide will not be at the forefront of people's minds. There is just the shattering realisation that the one who was so alive is now dead. At this moment, nothing has relevance for the family but the devastation they are feeling. This is palpable as you enter the home or the scene of the suicide. The family in their state of shock must be respected and we, in our pastoral or friendship capacity, should not feel that we have to know what to do immediately. Nothing we can say will connect until we are in some sort of communion with the bereaved. From this earliest stage of an unfolding tragedy, the pastoral carer can only lay the foundation of empathy and support by trying to enter in some even small way into the world of the bereaved. There is a value in just being present for the bereaved. There is no need to know all the answers; it is important just to listen and take cues from those present.

This truth came home to me over twenty years ago when I lived in a parish in San Francisco. The cook in the parish house was diagnosed as HIV positive. None of us priests had any real knowledge of what to say and how to approach this young man. Our words were inadequate and didn't prove helpful. It was clear that the only one who seemed to be reaching him and helping him was a lady, a great-grandmother, who was the housekeeper. She talked to him and he often went to chat to her. Finally, I asked her how this was working out so well. Her answer was blindingly simple: she asked him what she could do for him. His answer was equally simple: hold me and hug me. She entered into a real human communion with him. I, and maybe some of the other priests, lacked this ability of communion.

Let me give another example. One bright Sunday afternoon, I was asked to go to a house some distance from where I lived in Belfast. When I arrived, there were a large number of young people out on the street, speaking in hushed tones. They seemed to be everywhere – at every gateway, sitting on the kerb and leaning against cars. What was noticeable was the almost total lack of sound. As I made my way into the house I got a few nods and I could sense their eyes on me. The front room was packed with people. The coffin was in the window space. A young woman was sitting on a chair weeping her heart out, with her hand on those of the young man in the coffin. Apart from her sobs, there was silence. Nobody spoke a word except to offer me a seat. There we sat, in total silence. At the beginning, I felt so uneasy. Shouldn't I as a priest know what to say and do? I didn't. It gradually came to me that I was the least qualified in that room to say or do anything because I knew hardly anything of what had happened. I had just arrived and I could only presume that the other people in the room were family, relations and neighbours.

After what seemed an eternity, but what was probably less than half an hour, I picked up the 'message', the 'vibe' from those in the room, which seemed to say 'we are all lost and we too don't know what to say or do'. I was glad that I hadn't rushed in with words or suggestions as soon as I arrived. Even an expression of sympathy could have been out of place.

It was impossible to be sure that I had picked up the right vibe, but I got the sense of what was happening. It was worth taking some initiative, even though I was an outsider to this scene of terrible grief. Gently and quietly, I asked if we should say a prayer for the deceased young man and those who were heartbroken at his death. Without saying a word, people began to drop to their knees in readiness to pray. Far louder than the noise of knees hitting the ground was the sigh of relief – we were going to do something at last. In the Catholic context, we prayed a decade of the rosary.

When the prayer ended, people sat back in their seats as before. What I had not realised was the number of young people from the street who had gathered around the door as they heard the murmur of prayers being said. Now that the silence was broken, tea and introductions were made and the sequence of events leading to the discovery of the young man was gone over many times and in great detail. The lovely young woman at the coffin joined in and told her story.

Clergy, in particular, may find it difficult to let the words of the family, or their silence, indicate where they are in the aftermath of a sudden death, especially that of a suicide. A long time after this happened, I took part in a television discussion on suicide and mentioned this need to wait for people to let you know what is happening. The following Monday morning, a priest phoned me to say that when I made this observation he didn't think there was much sense to it. However, the very next day he was called, for the first time in his ministry, to the home where the suicide of a young person had been discovered. As he went into the house, he felt so inadequate and afraid that he might not have the right words to offer. He recalled what I had said and so he just sat down until the situation became clearer to him. By the time he did speak, he had a much better idea of what might possibly be helpful.

Attending to the Grief-Stricken

Presence, physical and emotional, is the essence of the pastoral response in these circumstances. Bit by bit there grows an awareness of the myriad, turbulent emotions of the bereaved. Shock, numbness and denial are part of the first heart-wrenching wave. There is a sense that this cannot have happened – it can't be him; it can't be her. 'There must be some mistake' is the hope that is put up as a defence against the truth of what has just been learned. This can be followed by a comment about when the dead person was last seen and how they looked or behaved. If sickness or depression were factors, someone might say that no one could have seen it leading to this. Some people physically run away because it is just too much. I remember seeing a mother run when she saw me walk towards her house following an all-night search for her missing son. As she passed me on the narrow path, she simply shouted, 'It can't be true. It can't be him'. She was gone and it was only later that I could meet her and listen to her pain and desolation.

I have frequently been asked if, at this early stage, we should use the word 'suicide' as we begin engaging with the family. There are deaths that are interpreted from the beginning as a suicide and we should never be afraid to name 'suicide' when this is clearly the case. However, talk of suicide right away is not always helpful. This will come later and gradually. It is my experience that it is better to wait and listen for the language the family use to describe the death. Some will openly talk about a suicide having taken place. Others will use roundabout ways of describing this sudden death. In some circumstances, there may be a lack of knowledge as to whether suicide or an accident is the cause. The family will in their own time talk about what they believe happened and then it will be possible to relate to the death as a suicide.

All deaths leave a huge gap and some of the emotions and reactions mentioned above will occur as part of the grief response. In the aftermath of a suicide, there are additional factors. As well as the numbness and denial, some of the bereaved will lash out in anger at what this person has done. It is as instinctive as the running away reaction and says nothing about the real love and affection felt for the deceased. It is just impossible for them to comprehend and piece together what has happened. At this point, the pastoral carer may have to act as something of a lightening conductor for the grieving person, family or community. The anger and distress has to go somewhere. Such strong emotions may also become self-directed and turn into feelings of guilt, as the suffering family berates themselves for failing to anticipate this conclusion. Some may ask themselves, 'What does this say about me and my family?' which can then lead to feelings of shame. All this is normal. The main response at this stage will be to listen and allow the bereaved to express whatever they need to express.

Another response to death by suicide may be silence: there is so much to deal with, so much happening, and there are so many unanswered questions. It seems almost futile to start a conversation with anyone and so a deep silence can rule. The bereaved don't know what is going on in their hearts and minds, and often feel incapable of articulating anything. This needs to be respected. The bereaved should not be hurried. However, it is important that the pastoral worker be alert to the person who withdraws. This needs to be monitored because the interior world can haunt a person and bring them into places from which it is not easy to leave without serious damage. At the scene of every sudden death, and particularly that of a suicide, everyone who can should try to watch out for the signs of a person who withdraws. Just be there for the person should they wish to test the waters of talking. Even a little opening up can prove critical in such moments. It is not helpful, of course, to have people feel they are being observed and shadowed at every turn, so sensitivity is crucial.

Following a death by suicide where church allegiance or religious practice are not evident, there is still the same need to 'listen' to the silence and to the words, to 'read' the situation and be ready to offer some initiative by way of words or actions. It always seems acceptable for the latest person who arrives into the house to eventually ask what happened once you have judged that it is safe to take this risk. Risk it is, because you never know for sure whether people are ready to talk or not. However, time and time again, I have found that people welcome the chance to tell and retell the story. It is almost therapeutic for those closest to the one who has died to have another chance to tell it once again. It may be that the best you can do is to be present, to accept tea or to assure the people that their loved one will be in your prayers. It is important to respect the religious beliefs or absence of such, so the mention of prayers can be put in such a way as to reassure the relatives and friends that you are doing this because you want to share with them this awful loss.

In the aftermath of a suicide, we are in territory for which there is no map and very few signposts. The common denominator may not always be religious belief but humanity in pain binds us incredibly closely together. It is interesting that in the Passion of Jesus, when all but a few of those chosen by him had deserted, it was a Roman soldier who proclaimed, 'This truly was the Son of God' (Mark 15:39) What he saw in Jesus was not his teaching but his tremendous love to the point of death on a cross. When we remember that Jesus took flesh and became one of us, we will always be close to those who are going through their passion and know what it is to be crucified.

Breaking the News to Children

Often, the first on the scene of a suicide will be a family member, neighbour, colleague or member of the public who may come across what can be a gruesome scene. Very quickly there will be police, ambulance service, doctor, clergy, undertaker and others. Response will also come from neighbours who are immediately sucked into a situation that may be completely new to them. Word spreads so fast because of mobile phones and soon the news has to be broken to family members who are not close by.

If the discovery is made by a child or children are present at the scene, some issues arise very quickly. The importance of listening is key in this circumstance, to hear what the child is saying – and not saying. Each child will have their own way of putting a 'shape' on death, so it is crucial to talk to them and find out what they know and don't know about death. This will allow you to judge how to help them cope better.

Children are great observers but, because of their young age, they may not be very good at interpreting events. Children miss very little and notice small changes in adults' attitudes. They will immediately know that something serious has happened. They will see relatives, friends and strangers gathering, talking and shedding tears. Some of these people will be in uniform and may arrive in police cars and ambulances. To small eyes and hearts this must be frightening. The child may be taken to a relative's house in the immediate aftermath of the discovery but their questions will go with them and will not disappear.

When dealing with children in these situations, bear in mind that age and development are factors that influence how they perceive what has happened. A pre-school child will have seen cartoons in which their favourite character is killed or injured, yet in the next episode that same character is back – fully alive and unscathed. While children do not live in a fantasy world, they can see death as reversible and temporary. At an older age they will come to know that death is final, though they may not yet associate it with their own lives. As the child moves into adolescence, they will realise that not only is death final and irreversible, but it is also personal: one day they too will die. Listening to children talking among themselves will reveal these different stages of understanding.

A pastoral carer arriving on the scene following a suicide may well be asked what the children should be told or if they should be moved away to stay with relatives. There is no one answer to these questions. Those who know the child best will be able to tell the pastoral carer the stage of understanding they believe the child has reached. In the light of that understanding and having talked to the child about the one who has died, a plan for the coming days can be put together.

As always in the area of death and, in particular, suicide, the language used to talk to the child will be important. To explain that the loved one has gone to heaven may be sufficient as a first response where there is a religious background in the family. Even the pre-school child may be familiar with being in a church and possibly church services such as Mass. Children attending school will already have been introduced to religious ideas such as angels and saints, and some of these may be of help.

It is important not to use words that may increase the child's insecurity. For instance, in the Liturgy for the Dead, prayer is offered that the person 'rest in peace' and enjoy 'the sleep of the just'. In that context, such language is both appropriate and comforting. However, these words may cause the child to worry that a parent or someone close to them who goes for a 'rest' or a 'sleep' may not come back. Common sense is the best indicator and most families have their own way of dealing with reassuring their children.

If the family into which the pastoral carer arrives does not have a religious connection, it is important not to introduce religious terms without any explanation or preparation. If children are present who have not been introduced to religious practice, such new language may be confusing, even frightening, for the little ones to hear.

Keeping the child's trust by being truthful and using words they understand will help create a better future for the child. In the days ahead, there will be so many new happenings for the child that their needs should never be neglected. In years to come, some children will have questions to ask surrounding the events of the death and funeral. As all parents know, the child will hear other children talking about the death and may need reassurance that they and others in the family are safe. There is no way of shielding a child from this. But the care at home and the readiness to listen to them and answer their questions will go a long way to creating a safe and secure environment for the child. It may also give the parent or other adult an opportunity to further think through their own thoughts and reactions to what has happened.

Family members should not be surprised to find themselves lost about where to turn for help in trying to do their best in this new and bewildering situation. There is help available. Cruse (*www.cruse.org.uk*) is a charity specialising in bereavement. Founded in 1959, it is contacted by 80,000 people each year for information. (Even this figure helps us know that we are not alone in being unsure what to do). The name 'Cruse' comes from a lovely passage in the Old Testament (1 Kings 17:12) about a widow's jar of oil (called a 'cruse') that never ran out. From this image the message is given that support will never run out as long as it is needed. That is a wonderful and powerful reassurance when the challenge following a suicide seems too great. Even though Cruse has this biblical background, it is a non-religious organisation which welcomes people of all shades of belief and none. One of their publications that could be consulted regarding children is *Has Someone Died?* There are other organisations too (see pp. 103 and 107–8) but the main point is that help is out there.

It is truly amazing how swiftly a family finds itself plunged into this territory of suicide and its issues. From never thinking a suicide would come to their door, they are suddenly faced with arrangements to be made and questions without any easy or obvious answers. In the next chapter, we will begin to explore how these can best be dealt with.

Chapter 2

Formal Procedures and Emerging Questions

There is no rehearsal for the death of a loved one. This is particularly evident when suicide is the cause. There can be no preparation and the normal points of reference are lost. There are no nightly visits to the hospital or hospice. There is no gathering around the bedside of someone who is slowly slipping away. There is a sharp break with all that was familiar and taken for granted.

This chapter will go through the very difficult moment when the body is removed for the post-mortem examination. Family and friends may find this unbearable. The most important thing is to be aware of the emotional state of the bereaved, letting them know that you are there for them if they need you, without giving them the idea that they are being watched.

This chapter will also approach the frightening phenomenon of copy-cat suicides, where those bereaved by suicide have died shortly after by suicide, leaving us to wonder if there is a connection. We will then discuss the issue of trust and confidentiality, and how ultimately the safety and well-being of the person must be the priority for the pastoral carer.

Formal Procedures

If the suicide has taken place at home, one of the toughest moments can occur when the body is to be removed. In this context, an undertaker will arrive for the removal to a mortuary so that the required post-mortem can take place. It is not a pleasant sight: it may not be the familiar hearse and coffin but rather a van with a long shelf in the back. This can come as a shock. I have often suggested that family members who would prefer not to see this be absent as it unfolds. It can be the case that some family members will join the priest or minister for a prayer before removal, while others go into another room until it is over.

At this time, it is essential to exercise great respect for the family's wishes. There is no one fixed rule for all, as family and individual needs vary so much. My experience has been that those responsible for this removal to the mortuary act in a most sensitive and helpful way. They, too, are affected by the situation, no matter how often they have been called to previous deaths by suicide. Recently one of these people remarked on how often over the past few years we had met in these circumstances and how it never gets any easier.

Police will be involved at this time and they will require statements from family members as soon as they are ready to speak. Police have a difficult role to play in the aftermath of a suicide. They are officers of the law and are not there to make it difficult or awkward for the family. Over the years, I have found that the attitude of the police officers can be important in these early hours. I have witnessed officers who were of enormous support to the family and others who were clearly there just to do a job and no more. It can sometimes be forgotten that some of the scenes to which emergency services are called make a deep impression and have a great impact on those men and women. Some of them may have a parent, a brother, sister or child of their own who is the same age as the one whose life has ended by suicide. Others will have memories of relatives or colleagues who died in this way. I have seen members of the emergency services shed tears of sorrow because of what has happened.

It can happen that members of the immediate family may not have arrived at the place where the suicide occurred before the removal to the morgue. In some instances, they may ask to go there immediately to see the deceased loved one. There is no denying this request and sometimes a member of the clergy may be invited to accompany those going on this sad journey. On arrival, it is important to prepare the relatives that it will not be easy for them to see the one who has died in this situation. People's first reaction is usually to cradle or hug the deceased. It can be the case that touching the person is prohibited until certain procedures of the post-mortem have been carried out, but it is very difficult not to reach out and hold the one who has so suddenly been taken away in death. There is no easy answer to this conflict, but understanding and appreciation on both sides usually leads to a resolution.

One small crumb of consolation for the relatives is to remind them that soon enough the deceased will be back to the family for the time of the wake, or whatever arrangement they choose to make. This will not take away the urgency of wanting immediate contact. But it will help them appreciate that the grieving is only beginning and that there are a number of days ahead in which many moments of real close contact and caring can be shown. These moments are in the context of traumatised people who are struggling to make any sense out of what has just happened. When assisting the family, one cannot expect too much from people. Once you realise this, there is less chance you will expect too much.

Why Did This Happen?
No matter what the sequence of events, there comes a moment when questions are asked that may have been in many a mind and heart about the suicide: why did this happen? Why did he or she die by suicide? Was there no other way? Could I have spotted it and done something? Am I to blame? This is especially the case if there has been an argument or falling out just before the suicide.

The question, if not the answer, as to why the person died as they did can emerge in some instances when family, friends or neighbours begin to recall the last time they saw the deceased. Often it will be remarked on how well and happy the person looked. There can be the bewildering fact that the one who died had booked a holiday just recently. The person may have spoken about their plans for their birthday or special occasions, such as Christmas or Valentine's Day, giving no clues about how their death by suicide was close at hand. The question of why this happened will continue to surface, both directly and indirectly.

It is so important that we learn as much as we can about this increasingly common reality of suicide in our midst. There is a lot already known and a lot that we don't yet know. There are many fine groups who dedicate themselves to research and analysis in an effort to eradicate suicide. Universities have been proactive in taking on academic studies, as have medical schools and practitioners. Political parties have held events to highlight the reality of suicide in society. Schools have welcomed groups in to speak to their pupils on the issue, as it is likely that so many second-level pupils will have come across suicide in their own family, school or among their friends. Every possible means should be explored to assist research and prevention programmes, to recognise potential warning signs and to prevent death by suicide.

However, when all this is said and rightly applauded, I am convinced that no full and final answer can be given as to why this person died in these circumstances, often without any discernable warning. Nobody close to one who has died should blame themselves for not recognising what was going to happen. While vigilance is important once we are aware that someone may be at risk, if we took every sign of low mood, every broken relationship, every taking of drugs, every binging on alcohol, every piece of news of a serious illness as a sign of suicide, we would be forever watching each other for signs of suicidal intention.

When a suicide has happened and those closest to the deceased try to piece together the clues and indications, I am convinced that the one who died carries with them into eternity a secret that is uniquely theirs. It is like seeing their life as a mosaic with all but one piece before us. We can know so much about the one who died but they have taken with them something that is theirs, something that we could not have known. For a believer, the knowledge of this uniquely personal reason for the suicide will be known only in eternity. We may be greatly surprised as to what it was that ultimately led them to suicide.

Sometimes people ask if the one who has died left a note or anything that might give an indication as to why such a final solution as suicide was seen as the only way for them. In some instances a note or a letter may be found. However, there is no guarantee that this note or letter will fully explain why this has happened.

I recall once where a man left a ten-page letter to his wife so that she could have something to tell their little child who was still too young to know what had happened to Daddy. The police took this letter away as evidence but, quickly enough, at her request, gave her a copy of this precious and sacred document. She asked me if I would read it with her. I suggested that she do so on her own out of respect for her privacy and because neither of us knew what might be in it. But when she insisted that I be with her to read it, I agreed.

We sat down with no one else present and began to read it out loud. It was heart-rending to hear what he had written. Both of us shed tears. Page after page brought fresh pain and anguish to his beloved wife. Even though my relationship with the couple was not that close, I could feel the pain on both their parts. It was an extraordinary experience to know that this had been written to be read soon after the death this young man was planning. It was with relief when the final page was put down. We sat there together in silence for some time. The wife then turned to me and asked if I now understood why her beloved husband and father of their child had died as he did. Truthfully, I had to answer, 'No'. After a short pause, she simply shook her head and said that neither did she understand. It was a beautiful letter and one that moved me deeply, but it brought home to me that the 'why' of a suicide is far from easy to answer. Not having an answer to the 'why' question is not an admission of despair but a profound respect for the loved one and their secret.

To the person who plans to die, there are issues and worries that can grow out of proportion. When these concerns get out of perspective, suicide has its own logic. In the suicidal mind, alternative solutions appear absent. The only way out seems to be to say goodbye to those most loved. The letter is meant to 'explain' to those who matter most why this loved one ended their life. Those left behind often question why their beloved could not speak to them of their pain and desperation. This letter revealed to me how extreme pressure, worry, depression, feelings of failure, financial worries or other reasons can distort the mind and heart, making suicide seem the only solution. All or some of these worries can be present in others who do not become suicidal. It is a mystery that defies a full explanation.

The mystery of what brings a person to their death by suicide alerts us not to judge those who took the path of suicide just because it does not add up in our estimation. For that young man, suicide seemed the only answer. He had the foresight and composure to write a long letter to those he loved most. In the absence of an immediate explanation of a death, surviving family members, close friends and others linked to the one who has died must be cherished and cared for at this vulnerable moment as the thought of suicide may cross their minds as somehow being worthy of imitation. There is a need for sensitivity in doing this so as not to give them the impression that they are being watched all the time. The cherishing and caring must respect the individual temperament of the person while being there for them should someone be needed. There can even be a danger that other people may use the suggestion of someone being suicidal in a hurtful and damaging way.

'Copy-Cat' Suicides

There is much debate about 'copy-cat' suicides. I am no expert, but I do know that people have died by suicide very shortly after the suicide of a close friend or family member. An important factor in preventing suicide within a group of friends is how the initial suicide is portrayed and reported by media outlets. Any form of glorification can sow the seed of perhaps following the same path, especially in the mind of a young person.

Where the person who has died by suicide was still in school, the immediate provision of counselling can help the school deal with students who may be experiencing suicidal thoughts. It is never possible to be with vulnerable people all the time, but where the school has concerns, it is important that parents be alerted. The doctor also has an important role in the aftermath of a suicide, so that when referrals are made they are aware of the background situation. It is not possible to identify all who may be tempted to follow along the road to suicide but the more a community becomes involved, the better chance of preventing further deaths and attempted suicides.

There are training courses, some of them of one or two days' duration, which can enable those within a community to identify some of the warning signs of suicide and to provide better support to the bereaved. I don't believe that it is possible to give a definitive answer on how much the first death led to the second. However, listening to the conversations of the bereaved following a suicide, I have to suspect that there is a connection.

For a child to want to follow a parent who has died by suicide is understandable, especially in a situation where religious belief tells us that we will meet again in eternity. I have been asked if it would not be right to go after the parent, brother or sister into eternal life and be with them for ever. In the intensity of grief, the pull can be so strong and the answers so difficult to find. The only response to those distraught is that this would not be best for them or those left behind. At this moment of loss, only in the embrace of love and the giving of security will it be possible to help another hold on to life and believe that it is right to go on living. Sometimes, suggesting that life could be lived in memory of the one who has died offers a little comfort.

Confidentiality – and When to Break It

One of the great acts of trust is when a person trusts another human being enough to confide their worries and concerns to them. This can be within a family context, among friends or in a caring setting. The matters confided in any setting are of fundamental importance to the person who is upset or worried. They may seem less serious to the person listening but that is not what matters most.

It can happen that we find out that a person has the intention to die by their own hands. The shock of hearing this is not easy to absorb. It also immediately presents a dilemma for the one who has received this information. It is sometimes said that the person who talks about dying by suicide does not intend to do so or will not do so. This can be a dangerous assumption, as it has been shown that in many instances this is not the case.

When danger of suicide is present, the most urgent need is to keep the person safe and to get help and support – or at least indicate to the person where these may be found. A key element for volunteer members of suicide prevention groups is to have support on hand when such an emergency arises. A suicidal person may refuse all offers of help and support. They may have found it difficult enough to tell another person how terrible their life has become and how bleak the outlook is for them. There is a great dilemma as to how to help the person without breaching their confidentiality and destroying whatever trust they have built up in another person.

Each situation differs and no one-for-all way of helping can be relied upon. Where life is in danger through suicide, a way of preventing this happening has to be found even should it mean breaking a confidence received. This is not said lightly and may seem a wrong approach to some people. Where the setting allows, the confidentiality aspect is best mentioned and explained to the person at the earliest possible stage.

As said so often elsewhere, it is important to listen to the suffering person who is feeling so desolate and lonely. Gently and kindly, it is important to find out who is available to help whether it is family, friends, spouse, social worker, doctor or teacher. If there are friends or family members already with the distressed person, they can be of immense help. The ideal outcome to the dilemma of preserving confidentiality is when the person themselves allows another to be approached for help.

We do not live in an ideal world. Sometimes, when the person won't or is not able to agree to contact anyone, there arises a duty of care to make contact with next of kin, GP or some other helping service. In these difficult circumstances, it is important for pastoral carers to have their own help and support. This is a huge amount for a person to carry on their own shoulders. The pastoral carer needs support and encouragement in what is a matter of life or death of another human being.

It has been my experience that friends or family members of the suicidal person have been of immense help and support. This is particularly true if the emergency arises in the middle of the night or at a time when medical and other social support services are not as readily available.

In the area of dealing with information received about a suicide being likely, there can be legal obligations to be observed. Where a carer is part of an organisation, statutory or voluntary, it is essential to be aware of legal requirements. In an age of increasing litigation, outcomes of any legal action have to be taken seriously. A code of best practice for dealing with information is needed in organisations for the sake of those working in the area of suicide prevention.

The seal of confession is absolute. Should a priest hear of an intended suicide in this forum, every effort will be made to invite the person to talk of this outside of a sacramental confession. In the event that all such efforts of persuasion fail, then the priest is faced with the bleak prospect of being rendered powerless to act in preventing what is threatened. Fortunately, such a stark dilemma would, in my pastoral experience, be rare. A priest will always continue searching for a way to preserve a life while not violating the seal of confession.

In exploring these issues and the persistent question as to why the person died as they did, it is important not to lose sight of the state of shock in which these people are trying to focus on a whole range of issues. Funeral arrangements and the dread of letting the loved one go still remain to be faced. The next chapter will deal with how the pastoral carer can offer support in the days surrounding the funeral or cremation, and how they can work with the family to create a personal, meaningful yet appropriate funeral Mass.

Chapter 3

Saying Goodbye

Until a person has experienced the desolation at the moment of loss, it is impossible to know how awful it is and how desperate you can feel. It is almost like being among people speaking a foreign language – if you don't know their language, you won't know what they are saying. The language of the broken heart is unique and does not translate easily. There is no dictionary in which you can find the meanings.

However, while we can never presume to fully understand what another is going through in their grief, we can try to intuit by attending with love and care, and having the patience to wait and listen until we become aware of what might be happening. In the aftermath of a suicide, the experience of those early hours and days will be forever with the bereaved. Even when years have passed, the loss of a loved one can be felt as really and as intensely as it did when that loss occurred. It is a very delicate time and I would not like to give the impression that I know exactly what should happen. There is no one right way for the human heart to come out of shock and loss. To give the person the space they need to react as they choose, and not as I, or someone else, may think they should, is vital.

What is good to remember is that, while these moments will remain forever with the person, so too will the one who has just died. There is no doubt in my mind that at crucial moments in my life, I just knew my late mother was there for me. It was not a vision, it was not a voice, and it was nothing like that. It was in the world of the spirit that she was 'around', 'present' and having a powerful and positive influence. It seems to me that we have to let the loved go first and then wait for them to come back to us. They will come back, and whether we experience their presence or not, they are there for us and with us. But that dawning is a long way in the future.

This chapter will explore the days surrounding the funeral or cremation – placing a death notice in the paper, speaking with the undertaker and arranging the funeral Mass – and how each of these stages can arouse different emotions in the bereaved. It will look at the role of the pastoral carer in situations where the family has no religious belief. It will also offer advice on how to take the wishes of the bereaved for the funeral Mass into account, without ruining the liturgical celebration. It will end with a warning about the danger of unintentionally glorifying death by suicide, cautioning us that vulnerable people present at the funeral might see this death as a way of gaining some recognition and love.

Beginning the Leave-Taking
An immediate issue for the bereaved is that the loved one is going to be taken away for burial or cremation.

The pain of this comes at a time when the family and all associated with the death are at their lowest. It is likely that, since the death, they have got very little sleep or regular meals. There will have been no normality or routine to their lives. There is a sense in which time stands still and even knowing what day it is becomes difficult.

However, even though it might seem insensitive to broach this topic in the midst of the tragedy that has unfolded, it is important that they begin to plan the goodbye for the deceased. No two situations are alike and so the planning of the funeral and all that goes with it will depend on who, in the immediate family circle, is able to carry out the preparations.

A good way of beginning is by placing a death notice in the newspaper. In some cases there is just one insertion, while in others there will be multiple notices with very personal messages of sympathy and an expression of what the death means to those left behind. This can open a window of opportunity to begin gently raising the issue of the funeral arrangements. It takes real courage for the family to move into this territory – nobody wants to think of the final goodbye when the coffin leaves the house or funeral chapel.

There are sometimes factors involved that make for complications at moments like this. If the parents of the deceased have separated and are perhaps in other relationships, the sensitivities involved should be respected. Even arranging the location of a wake may take some negotiation. In these moments, friends, neighbours, clergy and others can be extremely helpful. Not being family in this instance can be a help because they are not involved in the 'politics' of any family situation. It will be a time of listening and testing out options and possibilities before agreement is reached.

A sensitive and understanding firm of undertakers can be of great assistance as plans for the funeral begin to emerge. The variation in families as to how they go about arranging the religious or other farewell to the deceased is as unique as each suicide. Where a bereavement support group of lay people and religious already exists in a parish setting, they can prove very valuable help in making a first approach about what might happen at the funeral. This can help the priest or minister to have the ground prepared and sometimes give the family an opportunity to check out what might or might not be likely to happen.

There are increasing numbers of families who decide not to have any religious service at all. Where this is the case, it is a good idea to visit the home of the bereaved as a neighbour in the locality and to offer your condolences. Without fail I have been welcomed. However, it is important not to use such visits to try to change the family's mind. Their wishes must always be respected.

In a world growing in secularisation, there is likely to be an increase in non-religious services of farewell. The important thing to remember is that the loss is just as great and the grieving just as intense. In fact, in the absence of a religious faith in the Resurrection, the challenges faced by the family may be even greater. If I was allowed to retain one tenet of faith to the exclusion of all others, I would hold on to the Resurrection and the promise of eternal life after death. In ministry, it has been a true blessing to be able to say to a family that their loved one is safe and that God is caring for them.

Planning the Funeral Service

In circumstances where a Mass or religious service is to be planned, immense understanding is required from the priest or minister in guiding the family towards planning a liturgy or service which will honour their wishes and needs while remaining appropriate to the church setting. On the one hand, the Catholic Church has in more recent times acknowledged the need to recognise suicide in liturgy and prayer. In its funeral rites, there are some beautiful and compassionate prayers for those who have died by suicide.

On the other hand, I have encountered concerns from families about what in earlier decades was a much less sympathetic attitude on the part of Church and State. While it will seem harsh now, there will be older people who will remember a time when the Church took a strong stand by not burying those who died by suicide in consecrated ground. There will be people who will remember that until comparatively recently, suicide was regarded as a criminal act. That is the reason why it is no longer appropriate, and can be hurtful to families, to speak of a person 'committing suicide'. Even though such matters may not be to the forefront of the bereaved person's mind, they are in the atmosphere of these early hours after the death. Great sensitivity, together with an awareness of the impact of such historical practices, is required on the part of the pastoral carer when the time comes to prepare the final farewell.

There has been some debate in recent times about the nature and format of a funeral Mass, particularly one following a suicide. People in a state of shock following their loss want to do the very best to provide a funeral that both captures something of the personality of the one who has died and expresses in some way how much they were loved. This is both right and beautiful. Hurt can result when the expectations of the family with regard to a funeral liturgy cannot be met. This can only be avoided by discussion, explanation and seeking agreement within the limits of what is possible in the context of a funeral liturgy.

Priests, dioceses and parishes differ in what is considered permissible for a funeral liturgy, irrespective of the cause of death. There can be unreasonable demands made of the priest or minister in preparing the funeral. It is always worth keeping in mind that music loved by the deceased can be played at the family home when a wake is held. In a funeral home, a request can also be made to have certain music playing as people gather to pay their respects. In the cemetery or crematorium, it is possible to have music played and words spoken by family and friends, together with the prayers of the priest or minister. By making people aware of these options, the possibility of hurt and disappointment can be reduced.

When these matters have been aired on radio phone-in programmes, it is sad to hear how so much hurt and misunderstanding has occurred. There is little chance of healing through a public discussion of what has happened. What a pity that some agreement was not worked out before it reached that stage. In situations where there is a pastoral worker or bereavement group who call to the home, it is possible to reduce difficulties that arise regarding the liturgy.

Points to Consider
In a church, as the funeral begins, it is crucial for priests or ministers to remember that before them are people crushed and broken-hearted by a suicide. The one who has died is there only in spirit. Every word spoken and every prayer offered is heard and remembered by the family, friends and congregation who have gathered. So, in a spirit of compassion, every effort should be made to avoid saying no to music, no to a poem, no to an item cherished by the deceased being brought up at the offertory of a Mass, no to any signs or symbols whatever.

Guidelines for celebrating any funeral within a diocese or particular parish are usually available at the time of preparing the funeral. Though moderation and recognition of the sacred character of the liturgy, particularly the Eucharist, are vital, severity is never a good pastoral approach. God will not be dishonoured or mocked by some accommodation to the situation of saying goodbye, especially following a suicide.

It is also important not to have one law for the clergy and another for laity. For example, at the funeral of a Passionist priest, on his coffin is placed his mission cross, the sign from his habit, rules and constitutions of the Congregation of the Passion, a stole, a chalice, a book of the Gospels and, in the old days, his biretta (a liturgical head dress). Is it not a bit uneven to have this for a priest and then deny any recognition of the character and life of a layperson who has died?

In the case of the young, signs and symbols are very important. One has just to look at websites such as Twitter or Facebook to learn this and see something of the mentality and outlook of the young.

The funeral of a bishop, politician or well-known person can be a wonderful celebration of life. There can be special arrangements made to accommodate visiting dignitaries and well-merited words spoken of their achievements. Nobody would deny that such occasions are fitting in the circumstances of society. It is necessary to remember, though, that in the sight of God, all are his beloved children.

There is very little that cannot be solved by honest and open dialogue and planning. Over the years I have learned so much about the emotions and feelings of the family and friends of a deceased person by engaging in discussion about how they see the funeral being celebrated. There are boundaries and limits without which a liturgical celebration would be ruined, but many of the requests made over the years following a suicide have been relatively easy to accommodate.

Word of Caution

It must be ensured that suicide is not glorified through the celebration of the liturgy as if it was an admirable course of action when life is tough and there seems no other way of dealing with life's issues and challenges. As you look at the faces of young people going into the funeral of a friend, it always worries me that there may be some there who are wondering if this might not be a way out for them. The huge crowds, the music, the wreaths and flowers, the tributes, the tears of so many, the intense emotions. Observing all this, there may be a young person who feels that their life does not amount to much at this particular time. If suicide is presented in any way as a good option for dealing with the problems of life, a vulnerable young person may begin to wonder if this would be a way to get a bit of acknowledgement, affection and love. A lonely person, feeling unloved, may wonder if this would be a way to get sorely needed recognition and warmth. The funeral must never hold up suicide as such a good option. The message must always be that God calls us to the fullness of life and not to death. The balance is needed between holding firm to the sanctity of life while recognising how frail any of us can be under pressure.

Chapter 4

May They Rest in Peace

Saying goodbye is part of life and the final goodbye is spoken at death. Where a suicide has occurred many people have said how they would have loved one last chance, even a few minutes, to express love and affection. But the day of the funeral dawns and there can be a sense among the family that they cannot face letting the loved one go from them.

When a religious ceremony is to take place, the priest or minister can play a vital role by being present at the house early on the morning of the funeral. This is best done by arrangement with the family members. The primary purpose of being there is not in the first place to say prayers but simply to show human solidarity at a time of almost unbearable grief. The *Stabat Mater* used at the Stations of the Cross, especially on Good Friday, captures the mood. As Mary stood as mother at the foot of the Cross and watched, so the family this day are in truth on Calvary. This is the rawest expression of the Cross and it is wrong to try to disguise this. There is no shielding a person from this moment that is unlike any other.

This chapter will go through the difficult moments around the time of the funeral: being with the family as the deceased is moved from the home to the church, welcoming the one who has died into the Father's house. There will be some advice on what to include in the funeral homily and how to answer questions from the bereaved regarding mortal sin and heaven and hell. Another issue will be the situation where an explicit religious belief may not be a feature of celebrating the funeral. No matter what their beliefs, people need some kind of a ritual of parting.

Leaving the Home

People need a bridge to help them cross over from the days of the wake, when the loved one was physically present, to this moment of letting go and goodbye. I have found that a gentle recitation of the prayers of the Church for the journey from home to church can be helpful, but it is never going to make things easy. People need to ritualise in some way this moment of letting go. I have found in a religious context that a decade of the Rosary can be another form of creating that bridge to letting the loved one out of sight, though never out of mind. The prayers tell us that the loved one is safe in God's arms and will never again feel the pain that pushed them to ending their life. In the preface of the Requiem Mass, the family and congregation will hear the words: 'For your faithful people life is changed not ended.'

In situations where there is no religious service, the family will often decide that this is the time to play some of the deceased's favourite music. Some family member or close friend may have the strength to say something or recall times that were good with the one to whom they are now saying goodbye. This can be a way of creating an atmosphere whereby the dreaded moment of departure can be approached. There may be a favourite photograph, a drawing by a child, a football scarf, indeed almost anything that helps the family and friends to bridge the terrible reality of letting go.

It is important to remember that even where no religious service is desired by the family, God is still present among these suffering and broken people. It is not necessary to say this explicitly, but if believing members of the family or close friends ask if God is absent, reassure them that God being present does not depend on us but on Him. This can help a believing member find peace and reassurance that the deceased is not abandoned by God. It is part of being the People of God that we carry each other's sufferings, especially when the road is tough. It is worth looking into our own experience and remembering when believing might have been tough for any of us due to a death or tragedy. It is the faith, hope and, above all, love of others that carries us through.

It is not always possible to reach out in faith and prayer to those who have not shared this journey within a believing community. It is important to respect any requests about the nature of the funeral. For the believer, there is the great hope of eternal life, not only for our companions in the way of faith and worship but also for those who tried to live good and moral lives. I like to think of the wonderful final judgement scene in St Matthew's Gospel (25:31-46) when people are shocked to hear that they ministered to Christ during their lives without it being known to them. When did they see Christ a stranger, hungry, thirsty, naked, sick or in prison and minister to him? The wonderful answer is that as long as we did it to one of those around us, we did it to Jesus. It is my firm belief that there is no funeral where God is not a mourner.

There soon comes that dreaded moment when the final goodbye, the final kiss, the final hug comes and the lid must be placed on the coffin in the house or funeral parlour. There is not a word or a phrase to capture these final moments but if you look into the eyes of the family and catch their whispered words, you get a glimpse of their pain. Earlier we spoke of numbness as being a characteristic in the aftermath of the death. Now that numbness often gives way to a rush of feeling. Some people cry out in anguish. Others shed tears that come from deep inside and are born of love and the pain of loss. There is almost disbelief that this is happening and that the one who such a short time ago was part of the lives of all these people is not going to be about any more. The smile, the familiar phrase, their knock on the door and all the familiar characteristics are about to leave us.

In either a religious or other form of funeral, the time to place the deceased into a hearse for the final journey arrives. In some places it is possible to walk part of the way to the church carrying the coffin.

There will often be a number of groups prearranged who will carry the coffin in turn. In this way, family and friends will feel that they are part of the saying goodbye. Female relatives and friends of the deceased should never be excluded from this act of respect and of service to the deceased.

At this point we feel we have come to the limits of language and expression. Everyone ministering will be most likely able to recall a moment in their own life when saying goodbye to a deceased loved one seemed beyond anything we had ever gone through before. It is good to now recall that moment and those feelings, not to talk about them but to give us a fellow feeling with what is happening to those all around us. This can save us from rushing in to try to ease or even take away the pain. You cannot, and the effort to do so will come across in a manner that is not understood. It takes real courage to just stand there ready to be 'used' by those around you or to be ignored by the grieving.

That is the role of the pastoral care person and it is a bit like that of John the Baptist. He was a voice but not the Word. All he could do was prepare the way for another whose sandals he was unworthy to untie. The pastoral carer is there not to tell of their story but to listen and appreciate the bereaved people's story.

You will never forget the scene as a mother says goodbye to her child (of any age), a spouse to a partner, a friend to a friend. But you will treasure the privilege that it is to be allowed stand beside and be part of such a farewell. No matter how many funerals a priest or minister may engage in during a year, for a family at this moment this one is all that matters. While this is true in the life of a priest or minister in celebrating baptism and weddings, there is some particular vulnerability at the time of a funeral that will be remembered for a long time to come. A kindness shown at this moment of death and funeral is never forgotten.

Then the funeral procession moves off either directly to the cemetery or to the church. Again the priest or minister must stand ready to receive and welcome this child of God into the Father's house. Listening, observing and assessing are the keys to understanding what is happening to this congregation of people who are traumatised and shocked. They may be feeling anger, resentment, bewilderment, confusion, love, loss, despair and emptiness. It is important to remember that some or all of these emotions will be present as the liturgy is celebrated.

The Homily
At any funeral, it would take the wisdom of Solomon to get the homily even nearly right. If asked to preach at a funeral following a suicide, is it important to try to have some meaningful contact with the bereaved relatives and others before the funeral. To preach at a funeral without this background is extremely difficult and leaves the priest or minister open to introducing unintended misunderstandings.

The homily may centre on the prayer, 'May they rest in peace'. A funeral is a handing over of the one who has died to God. The unresolved question as to why this person died by suicide may remain in the heart of the preacher and among the congregation, but with the help of our faith, we can hand this person over to God so that they may rest in peace. In this way, we are not as tempted to analyse or to judge. The person is safe in the arms of God and it is not for us to be judgemental.

Only God knows what the person who died was feeling: maybe they wanted to call attention to some intolerable situation in their lives; maybe their pain was so great they could not see any other solution; maybe they felt they were a burden on those nearest to them; maybe they had consumed alcohol and/or drugs to cope with the turmoil and pain, and in this state went through with their own death. They may have done what they did for a mixture of the above or perhaps even for reasons that no one knows.

When we are free enough to allow that the reasons for suicide are complex, then the thrust of preaching has to be respect, even though we do not agree that suicide is a solution. What is spoken by the priest or minister will depend on how accurately the preacher has heard and 'read' the family signals over the previous days, along with his or her ability to draw from the Word of God a message for his 'crucified' people. Making the link between Christ crucified and the 'crucified' people in front of the preacher at this funeral is a challenge.

The deceased can be recalled in the homily by drawing on items like their favourite football team, the music they liked or the nickname by which they were known. This is not just another funeral, another suicide in a long line. This is the funeral of a loved one, who was cherished in an utterly unique way. God made this person totally special and wanted them to live life to the full. Somewhere along the road, life became unbearable for them and their decision to end their pain by suicide has now become a nightmare for the family and community.

When preaching at the funeral, it is important to assure the family that blame cannot be placed on them; this person chose to end their life by suicide. In a situation where one partner ended a relationship and the other died by suicide, it is important not to imply that the surviving partner is somehow to blame. It is a tragedy and so unfair when years later a surviving partner is still being held responsible for the death.

They Are With God

'Is our loved one in Hell?' 'If they died in mortal sin must they be damned?' These are questions that the priest or minister can be faced with, directly or indirectly. The pain behind the questions is born out of love and fear. Love, because the bereaved would spare nothing to bring their loved one back, or at least make them safe. Fear, because even if religious practice may have slipped, they still want their loved one to be happy. It is the challenge of the homily to somehow address these areas of concern.

I have only one answer to offer in such a context – the loved one is with God. When a person comes to the decision to die by their own hands, they have reached a point where two of the traditional requirements for mortal sin – clear knowledge and full consent – are greatly diminished if not altogether absent. Even if we can establish that the person had clear knowledge of what they are doing by taking their own life, it is my belief that they saw their death as the most loving, caring and helpful thing they could do for those around them. Theological or moral issues about eternal salvation can be used as background by the pastoral carer if the question arises about where the deceased is now. The same applies to the homily dealing with this question.

I recall a situation in which a young man had died by suicide. He had been quite shy, yet over a period of a month he took his parents, nephews and nieces and other family members out for meals. He also bought them simple but thoughtful gifts. The family were delighted; this apparent show of interest and affection did not alarm or worry them in any way. The young man seemed to be coping well and showing signs of developing a more outgoing manner after a long battle with depression. When he took his own life soon afterwards, it became clear that this was his way of saying goodbye. A decision, once made, gave him a sense of peace and contentment. His internal battles would soon be over, he would deal with the 'demons' and find peace after many tortured years of struggle, but first he would show his love and affection for those closest to him.

Full consent comes from a clear mind. When I have listened to those who did not complete the suicide, the choice to end their own life was described as a 'driven' act, a compulsion. At that time, the decision seemed to give them a sense of freedom, though I would not see it as true freedom.

That suicide is wrong must always be held with true clarity. We should not understate this. At some funerals, I have openly appealed that no one else bring this grief to their family and community by following the same course of action. There will be instances when this may not seem appropriate, but it is necessary to be clear that family or friends are never helped by the death of one they love. The person considering taking their own life must be reminded that it always a tragedy for those left behind.

It is a good idea to remind ourselves frequently that it is to the broken, grieving and disconsolate family and friends that a homily is preached and not to the deceased. The purpose of a liturgy of saying goodbye is to gently lead the grieving family and all present into the mystery of death which for the believer leads to resurrection. Where a religious belief is not present, there still remains the need to walk these painful steps of saying goodbye. The desired outcome of every funeral is hope and peace when neither may be in great abundance.

Chapter 5

Letting Go

The time will come when the final parting will take place in the cemetery or crematorium. By this time, the better part of a week may have elapsed since the discovery of the loved one who has died by suicide. Physical and emotional exhaustion may have set in among family, friends, colleagues and the community. Some will retain a heightened awareness of all that is happening. Others may not remain in such an alert state. Some people dull the pain, and thus their senses, with alcohol and other drugs. No one need be surprised at these situations as each person deals with trauma in their own particular way. However, it is of help if the family members and those close to the deceased can be consciously and coherently engaged in this most sacred of moments. This is the moment when the family, the community, and in a religious ceremony, the Church, returns the deceased back to God. This person and temple of the Holy Spirit is being honoured in their final moment of presence on this earth by those who love and care about them.

This chapter will explore the final stage of letting go. It will look at the role of the priest or minister as a support during the funeral and subsequent burial or cremation. The value of faith during times of unimaginable suffering will also be discussed.

The Final Goodbye

It is almost impossible for pastoral carers to imagine the devastation and sense of loss that accompany these final moments, this final letting go. It is important to be there for the family and those who were close to the deceased. However, it can be difficult to know how to help, what kind of support to offer. It has been my experience that simple things can make a difference out of proportion to what might be thought.

If the body of the loved one is to be cremated, and if some of the bereaved family has not witnessed a cremation before, preparing them for each part of the ceremony can help them avoid feeling shocked or upset by the proceedings. For example, there comes a moment in a cremation when the coffin slowly disappears from view. This is the last glimpse the family and friends will have of the mortal remains of the loved one and they might have questions about what exactly will happen to the body. A pastoral carer might consider arranging a visit to a crematorium to see how it works to be in a better position to respond to questions that may arise for the bereaved. Some of the stories that circulate about the cremation process can be easily dispelled by someone who has spent time observing the process from all angles.

Family and friends often stay on for some time in silence or with music playing in the background.

Sometimes they just don't want to leave the spot where they have seen their loved one for the last time.

A cemetery is generally more familiar to people – many will have been at a graveside before – yet the sense of finality as the coffin is lowered into the ground is just as great as in the crematorium. Where there is a custom of putting some soil into the grave, it is good to ensure that as many as wish from those present take their turn doing this. In some places, the immediate family, and especially children, will have a flower to put into the grave on top of the coffin as a sign of love and affection.

These and other local customs help the family and friends realise that the letting go is beginning to happen and that the journey ahead to a new relationship with the deceased is already beginning. There should be no rush to finish this part of the burial; standing around is part of the process of letting go. I recall seeing in Africa the grave being completely filled in before anyone moved away. This took more than an hour and gave those present an opportunity to talk and reflect on what had just happened. In some places in the past, there was the custom that women not go to the graveyard for the burial. Whatever is accepted in a particular community as a rite of letting go can be helpful to those who are not sure about the next step forward.

The custom exists among some to gather after the funeral for something to eat and drink. Sometimes people will drink alcohol – a long-standing tradition in many places that can give people the opportunity to reflect again on what has just happened. The loved one is gone and is no longer with us. People are only beginning to come to terms with letting their loved one go.

However, there is always the danger that alcohol may be used as an escape to continue to dull the almost unbearable pain that has been throbbing away in the heart for days. It would be harsh to condemn this behaviour, but it is clear that the issues around the death and the journey ahead without the deceased will still have to be faced at some point in the future. Most of these gatherings end quite well and people feel the support of those around them. Unfortunately, some end in violence and division because of what was said or done under the influence of alcohol, adding to an already tragic situation.

Going On
Nothing should surprise us in the area of suicide. Close contact with the aftermath of a number of suicides does not make me an expert in the pastoral care of those left to go on living. However, I have learned that it is important not to decide for the bereaved family what they are capable of coping with. I have been amazed and humbled by the sheer courage and strength of an already broken family.

One family buried their son on a hot summer's day. Nothing worse seemed possible. The rawness of loss and the pain of the one who had died were palpable each time I visited the family. Within a month, a second son of the family took his own life.

He had seen the devastation of his brother's death on his parents and siblings. He was broken-hearted beyond words. He was attentive to his parents and family in the immediate aftermath of the suicide of his brother. It was soon clear that he was under great strain. With good family and voluntary group support, he was receiving expert medical and therapeutic care. He was a good outgoing lad. He was a guest with his wife and child at a wedding that I celebrated on a Saturday afternoon. They were expecting their second child in the coming months.

He agreed when I spoke to him that the wedding reception would be tough as it was the first event at which his brother would not be with him. They had been very close. He told me that he knew it was going to be tough but assured me that he would be alright and would see his medical doctor in a few days. He had a family photo taken. That was the last time I saw him alive.

Next morning before 7 a.m. the police phoned me to say there was a person hanging from a tree not far from the church. One glance when I got there and I knew it was him. The suit, shirt and tie that had looked so good on him the previous afternoon were now his shroud.

His parents' house wasn't far away. The police agreed that I should break the news to the family. The front door was not locked. It was open for him. I called up the stairs. When the father came down and saw me he simply spoke his son's name. All I could do was nod. The words just wouldn't come out. We both knew that the agony of what happened just four weeks ago was now beginning again.

It is awful to imagine what must have gone through the hearts and minds of those parents on that Sunday morning. I had been privileged to grow close to them during the days following the first suicide of a son of theirs. Without disguising it, on that Sunday morning in that house with two sons dead within a month, I was broken in spirit and felt powerless. That is not all that relevant in comparison to what was going on in the family before my eyes.

It is amazing what people remember. That father remembered that I took coffee without milk or sugar because of the number of cups of coffee I had taken in that house over the past month. As we sat down at the kitchen table I knew that this again was Calvary. In the company of this family, I sensed that I was on holy ground as truly as the Cross of Christ is sacred. It is in moments like these that the lesson is learned that suicide alters forever the life of those left behind.

Standing beside, yet outside, of families bereaved by suicide, I have seen people finding the strength to begin the attempt to piece their lives together again. Even when in this instance two members were no longer there, the effort began and still continues. It takes heroic courage to resume the journey after tragedies that most of us can only imagine reverberate daily with some people.

A Sustaining Faith

Often I have heard people say that they could not go through something like the loss of two sons, especially in such a tragic way. In the family mentioned above, there was one factor that was evident on the occasion of each death. It was their faith in God. Earlier I said that it might be wise to be cautious about bringing God's name into discussion immediately. However, in this particular family, from the very beginning there was a solid faith that somehow pervaded all that was happening. God was seen to be present and active even in the midst of such horrific loss. This belief did not reduce by one iota the intensity of the pain felt or the loss experienced. It did not dry tears, answer why this happened or make it easier for the remaining siblings. That is not the purpose of faith in God. Their faith enabled them to know that there is a God who will see them through even this. It was their way of trusting that there was a foundation that would support them.

For a person who has fallen out with God because of their loss, these sentiments may give rise to cynicism or even anger. I have seen this reaction also among people of faith because they have been so deeply wounded by a suicide close to them. But where faith in God is active it proves a most wonderful support, without taking away the pain.

The other factor that sees people through is the support of family, friends and community. After a suicide there seems to be just two 'planks' that keep a family going: one is the tangible support of love from others and the other is the knowledge that even in this awful situation, God is not absent.

When this family had seen to all that was needed for the funeral of their second son they went shopping for a gift to thank me for what they saw as my support and help. That gift made me realise just how heroic people are in the midst of what is beyond the human mind to comprehend fully. Through events like this and others, I now know that resurrection takes place among 'crucified' people as truly as it did on Easter morning following Calvary.

Whether it is into a grave or the slow disappearance of the crematorium, the final letting go for the family and friends can only be very inadequately described by my words. Anyone who has witnessed this letting go will be humble and careful about what to say and do in the immediate aftermath of a death by suicide. Every time I see a hearse passing, even though I don't know whose funeral it is, I always offer a prayer for the deceased and one that the mourners be strengthened on this day of sorrow.

PART II

Chapter 6

Buses Run the Next Day

Once people have said 'goodbye' to the loved one who has died, they are faced with an empty space. After a death by suicide, a family and even a whole community can find it hard to accept that life goes on, perhaps feeling that there should be some acknowledgement of the enormity of what has happened.

The shock and suddenness of suicide will never leave the consciousness of the family and friends. In the days immediately following the discovery of the death by suicide, ordinary life was put on hold for those directly affected. People came to and left the house, church or cemetery – places associated with this different world in which the family and friends moved during those days. Quickly this 'new' world took on its own character, rhythm and pattern. The pastoral carer becomes part of this world of a family in transition, from saying goodbye to their loved one to beginning the experience of life without them. In my experience, this transition is never easy. I have learned from walking with families bereaved by suicide that the days following the funeral are painful and, in ways, feel unreal.

This chapter will explore the slow and painful journey that begins after the death of a loved one. While each family reacts to their enormous loss in a particular way, a common feature is that, sooner or later, all will attempt to engage again with the world they knew before the suicide. The world has not changed but people are profoundly different because of what has happened. A pastoral minister being aware of how challenging 'normal' life can be for the bereaved is better placed to offer support and advice as this journey begins.

Helping the Family Move On

With this as background, a visit from a pastoral worker immediately after the funeral is usually welcomed. There are so many things to talk about because so much has happened in such a short time. Even though unstructured, a visit or a number of visits can allow the bereaved to begin piecing together some of the events that may be confused or have been missed altogether. There is a need for the family to go back over these events in some way so that the life that lies ahead can have a thread of continuity with the past.

Every person is different as they take up life again and try to move forward. For some, reading cards and messages can be a source of comfort. For others, going back to activities with friends or relatives can help them piece together the recent past to help them move on.

The location where the suicide took place is important for the family and friends. If it was away from home, the family and friends may wish to mark in some way the place that will always hold such significance. In contrast, some may never wish to revisit the place again. Neither reaction is right or wrong.

If the death occurred at home, some families will decide to leave the house because the memories are too painful. The spot where the loved one was found serves as a daily reminder of the tragedy. It can trigger a re-living of the nightmare each day, with the feelings just as vivid as when the suicide actually occurred. The traces of the beloved are everywhere. There are photos, music, clothes, their bedroom; everything about the person is there. This heightens the sense of loss and profoundly changes the atmosphere in which the family lives. It is a new world where many of the previous landmarks have a different meaning. They speak of loss of what was once taken for granted.

Silence even brings back the memory of the loved one – their voice won't be heard again coming in the door, the particular way they knocked, the sound of their mobile phone, the way they were around the house. Family members can sometimes have dreams in which the deceased is alive – perhaps sitting together in the kitchen sharing a pot of tea – yet when they wake up, they are in a house that will never again be home to their deceased loved one. What is missing can be a powerful and painful reminder that the person is now no longer present. It may be the same house but certainly not as it was before the death.

On the other hand, there are families who decide that they will never leave the house precisely because of the presence of the loved one who died. It is a way of never forgetting and of honouring their memory. This creates for the family and those who regularly visit the home real closeness to the deceased that is part of the journey now beginning. Though life will never be the same again, it will go on.

Care is needed not to rush a bereaved person into full acceptance of moving back to normal life at once. Extra pressure is the last thing they need. Some people feel that it gets worse after the funeral. People say they feel strange, almost as if they are at one remove from what goes on around them. They might ask the pastoral worker if this will pass and if they will ever be alright again. There is no easy answer to this question because behind it there is a complex mixture of emotions. Perhaps the person is not so much seeking an answer as making a statement about their concern over the future. There are some people who feel that they will never recover and see only a bleak road ahead of them. Having walked beside such people, I appreciate their worry about coping with an uncertain future.

The pastoral carer will not help by suggesting to the broken-hearted person that they should be able to get their life back together again and move on. There is a need for the bereaved one to hear that how they are feeling is alright, and also that there is no pre-written timetable for the journey toward what was once regular life. The challenges on the journey to be travelled in the wake of the suicide of a loved one are known only to the grieving person. The pastoral carer can but seek to pick up a sense of what is happening in the mysterious world of the broken-hearted in the time following the suicide.

If the task for the pastoral carer or friends was solely to help the bereaved to return to what was there before, it would still be a huge challenge. But it is more complex than that. Every death creates a new situation for those left behind to mourn. The aftermath of a suicide shares this same truth, but maybe even more marked. The familiar points of reference that could be relied on before are changed since the suicide. What was there before may still look the same, but it feels different.

As examined in Part I, the question of why the person died as they did is never far away. The pain of loss can be intensified by wondering if the death could have been prevented. It is essential that pastoral workers hear this question and others that are there. The bereaved need the opportunity to explore what is happening in the aftermath of their loss. The pastoral worker must listen carefully before offering an opinion or suggestion. It is only by sensing what the grieving person is going through that it is possible to have any idea what the appropriate response might be.

Some in the immediate aftermath of a suicide go into long silences, speaking only when absolutely necessary. If this is how the person acts, it is important to accept it. For the pastoral carer to try to cheer the person up with conversation at these moments is likely to be as unsuccessful as it is insensitive. The pastoral worker can learn to listen within these silences. The silence of the bereaved person is as appropriate a response as is talking and asking questions. The discomfort with the silence may be more an issue for a pastoral carer than it is for the family member. Nobody should need permission or approval for silence.

It is very understandable that family members, friends and neighbours can be at a loss to know how best they can support and help those who are hurting so much. Life teaches us that there is no magic wand to take away the pain. In the first place, the message of being patient with oneself has to be given over and over again to the bereaved. The enormity of the trauma of discovering someone dead by suicide is hard to grasp and even harder to express. Some people are gifted in being able to draw near to the broken-hearted and strike a real cord of closeness and understanding. This can gently but powerfully reassure the bereaved that they do not face the future alone.

Children Returning to School
In the immediate aftermath of the funeral, there will be an effort to get back into the rhythm of individual and family life. Children go back to school. The school community may wish to mark the return to school of the pupil. It is likely that some of the staff

and perhaps classmates have visited the home and attended the funeral. If this is the case, then preparation for the return of the pupil to school will be a little easier. If that is not the case and there has been little or no contact with the family, great sensitivity will be needed. The school may meet first with a parent or other family member to plan how to ease the return to school of a pupil who has without warning gone through so much in a short time.

Many schools have access to a counsellor or have a link to a local counselling service. If the pupil shows signs of needing more than the school can provide, the parents should be asked if they would like to have their child referred for counselling sessions. It is fortunate that there is a far greater acceptance of counselling as part of a healthy life and that the stigma that used to be associated with it is now receding.

Teachers and members of staff can be well-placed to observe the pupil returning after a relative's suicide. Some younger children talk about the one who has died and continue to ask questions about where they have gone, what they are doing and so forth. Other children may enter into silence about their loss and say little if anything. Both of these situations, and all the shades in between, are normal. While respecting the child's silence it can be helpful to check out that the child is doing well in other ways – at play, class work, behaviour and general mood.

To assess what is going on in the life of an adolescent on return to school after a loss by suicide may be more difficult than with younger children. While respect must always be shown to the young adult, different approaches can be tried to initiate some conversation about their loss. But creating artificial situations to achieve this can have the opposite effect, with the young person closing up even more.

There are situations where the pastoral minister may be able to play a constructive role in becoming an intermediary between the school and the family. In my experience, where this is possible a lot of good can come of it. The school may be searching for a way to help the pupil but is looking for some family feedback. The family may appreciate a channel being opened up between them and the school which is where a pastoral carer can help. None of this is interference or meddling, but rather an honest attempt to help the young person come to terms with their world which has changed so much from what it was before the suicide.

Adults Returning to Work
Other family members must return to work. Their colleagues may have visited the home or attended the funeral. This can help a smoother return to work. Some will feel uneasy as the bereaved person comes back among them. This is understandable. Silence does not indicate indifference by colleagues but a difficulty in finding the words to say or the gesture to offer. The bereaved person, however, may not wish to have much said or done as they return to their work,

and such silences can be a welcome relief. Some larger companies may have in their personnel department resources to create a smooth return in these early days.

There will be bills to pay after the funeral. All the routine jobs and events of people's lives will be restarted. But it is not easy to have the heart to do this in the immediate aftermath of the loss. Some people find it extremely difficult to begin again but know that sooner or later a start must be made.

Every death has an aftermath. Following a suicide, there will be a repeat of all the elements family members have gone through during a previous loss. They know there are various stages to be gone through. But after a suicide, there are additional elements to go through. The loss is the same, the grief is the same but there is an almost indefinable element attached to a death by suicide. It is not easily captured. It is almost like a cloud that casts a shadow over the whole family and can reach into the heart of the community. A suicide is a death like no other.

The pastoral carer aware of this 'added' dimension in the aftermath of a suicide can try to build up a picture in their mind and heart of what is happening. This is no easy task. The tangle of cables around a television or computer is something of a mystery to me. Sometimes, I wonder if the interior life of the bereaved person may not be something similar. Each strand of emotion has its place but the trauma following a suicide leaves a 'tangle' of emotions and feelings that the person struggles to unravel and those around them are lost in trying to understand. For the pastoral carer to have an awareness of this complexity can save facile suggestions or quick solutions being put forward. Patience with how long it can be before the beginning of healing may begin is necessary for anyone who would wish to help and support.

Uncovering Hope

Following fourteen suicides in a small area of Belfast over a period from Christmas Eve one year to Saint Valentine's Day the following February, there was deep shock and worry among the people where they occurred. Public meetings were held not just to discuss the situation but to ask what could be done to prevent further loss of life. People who would not normally attend public meetings were to the forefront, offering constructive suggestions about how to cope with what was regarded as an epidemic. At that meeting, I had nothing more important to contribute than others there. But the presence of pastoral carers makes a statement concerning closeness to the community in a time of great need.

A pastoral worker can offer a lot by being present and active in such a gathering of people who are searching. They stand ready to offer practical help and support as avenues of action are suggested. Sometimes it may be by making contact with professionals who can help or by arranging suitable places where help and advice are available. An example of such activity may be organising a network of mobile phones where people agree to be 'on call' at certain times to assist as best they can. The list of what is needed is great and the pastoral worker can provide support and help.

After one of these meetings, a young person asked me if the area where all these suicides took place was cursed in some way. It was a sincere question which expressed a fear on the one hand and a desire to get to the root of what was taking place on the other. Responding to a question like this is never easy but it is possible to highlight the blessings that are present as well. I could reassure this young person that the community was basically healthy and blessed. It was possible to point out how many people, especially the young, had taken on a role of looking out for each other. The outpouring of love and affection for the families during the time of bereavement were signs of blessing. The practical assistance offered to care for the mourners and welcome with hospitality visitors to their home was another sign of real goodness. The number of cards and messages of condolence received along with the promise of Masses to be offered and prayers to be said were also a positive sign and one of blessing. Anybody, including a pastoral carer, who can offer this reassurance is giving a lot more to individuals and the community than they may realise.

In a community where suicides have multiplied, there is a palpable sense of fear that the situation is already out of control and could get worse. It is important for pastoral workers to offer grounds for hope. This does not mean downplaying the seriousness of what is happening and may continue to happen, but it does involve encouraging a positive stance in unearthing solutions and ways forward. People in a community become frightened by the gloom cast by even one suicide, never mind a series of them. The pastoral worker feels the pain also, but at the same time tries to offer hope. This may seem insignificant, but it is essential that people going through a whole range of experiences for the first time can find a pastoral carer who is there for them. It is often thought by pastoral workers that they are offering very little and doing very little. However, to stand firm and not lose hope is a gift to people who are struggling with what has happened and its consequences.

Another very practical sign of strength and recovery in any community affected by multiple suicides is when emergency action is planned and taken. Counselling can be organised and centres opened at weekends so that anyone feeling depressed or under pressure can access immediate help. Many will avail themselves of these services. Health authorities can publicise what help and assistance is available and groups such as the Samaritans make their contact details widely available.

Sustaining a Relationship
As every death is unique, so is every aftermath for the family and community. Not everyone will be affected in the same way. If a child or young person has died, the parents are profoundly altered. There are some parents who turn to each other and help each other

find a reason to move forward together. However, there are others who find resuming life together more difficult. This may give rise to serious strains on their relationship and can lead to breakdown. This is not anyone's intention, but because of what has happened, one or both partners may close off, excluding those closest to them. As well as the partner, the children in the family may also feel they are being kept at a distance. A pastoral worker coming into this situation need not be surprised if they meet marriage and relationship issues that are causing a new but very real suffering.

In their relationship, each party may be starting the post-suicide road from a different point. Both will experience loss, grief, disruption of family life, fears for the future among others, and each will have personal issues to work through. It can come as a surprise to one partner to discover how difficult they have been in the relationship since the death of the loved one. The other party may feel excluded from a world into which they appear to have no access. Though unintended, the hurt is real and can put enormous strain upon the relationship. In the end, some relationships survive and recover while others end in separation. Apportioning blame is not helpful. The pastoral worker needs to be aware that these strains and challenges often occur. To be able to help both parties separately and together is a real service to the family at this terrible time in their lives. Where this is beyond the competence of the pastoral carer, it is still of great assistance to indicate where help is available.

The impact of death by suicide is unlike any other loss. The aftermath for bereaved parents requires communication, even when this may be the last thing one or both feel capable of doing. Couples preparing for marriage are told how fundamentally important good communication is for the growth of the relationship. In the aftermath of a suicide, there cannot be enough emphasis placed on how crucial regular and honest communication will become. A partner may assume that the other knows what they are going through and how they feel. Mutual help and support is especially needed, and an absence of putting the blame on the other. The first time that other family members and friends sometimes learn of what has been happening in the couples' relationship is when separation is ready to take place. This comes as a total shock and adds to an already painful situation.

Great care must be taken by the pastoral worker not to see separation as a solution at an early stage following the suicide. The gentle encouragement of not giving up on communicating with each other can make the difference between the survival of a relationship or its ending. Judgement on either partner is not for the pastoral carer to make. The couple themselves may not know what is best and may need most of all a non-judgemental, sympathetic person near at hand.

Following the trauma of a death by suicide, not all people are capable of revealing their inmost thoughts and emotions, even to ones they love. It is no disgrace to admit that skilled help is needed. For pastoral carers, including clergy, to admit that they too are struggling to cope can offer encouragement to couples who are finding it tough. Very few of us can sort everything out by ourselves. We need others with a listening ear and a tender heart to help us express what is happening in our inner world. Any trace of stigma or perceived weakness associated with seeking counselling or therapy is, hopefully, a thing of the past.

The pastoral carer becomes aware of the weight of these demands on individuals and the family. It is essential for pastoral carers to see their role as being in co-operation with the bereaved and in support of them. It is a mistaken kindness on the part of helpers to see these burdens as theirs to carry. The pastoral carer can be a bridge builder and seek helpful ways of supporting and encouraging the gradual resumption of life by the family. The pastoral carer may be most effective when able to point to where help is to be found. Nobody has all the skills. To go beyond one's capacity renders the pastoral carer more obstacle than help in assisting others in sustaining and enriching their relationship.

Chapter 7

Some Challenges in the First Year

In the early weeks and months after the suicide, it is important for the priest and pastoral worker not to assume that the family and friends are coping well. For pastoral carers it is not always easy to keep up the contact with bereaved families, especially if there are a number of suicides around the same time. Sometimes an unplanned meeting with a family member or a short visit can be of great benefit to the family. It gives an opportunity for family to say how they are getting along. It may give an opportunity to share how awful life is for them and how little progress seems to have been made in coming to terms with what has happened.

This chapter will consider the milestones in the first year that bring back the intensity of the loss and examine some approaches to them. Every family and community has its own moments of significance. Every event, different this year due to their loss, will have great importance for the bereaved. These challenges of the first year cannot avoid reviving painful memories. The aim here is to see how pastoral carers can help with these great changes. While particular rituals or practices may be very different, all are aimed at bringing comfort. They can also mark the beginning of the healing of memories. Healing takes a long time and life will never return to what it was before. In all of these particular moments or events, pastoral carers are involved in a supportive role.

Month's Mind Mass

For many Catholic families the first big event will be the Month's Mind Mass. This is a custom in some countries. In eighth-century England, the Venerable Bede speaks of the day one month after the death as *'commemorationis dies'* or remembering days. From the sixteenth century, a collection of Sussex wills exists where a person expresses the wish to have torches burning at his month's mind. For many Catholic families the month's mind is important as it marks for them a chance to gather once more to remember their loved ones and to pray for them. That this remembrance gathering takes place a mere four weeks after the death means that emotions will still be very raw.

One month after the funeral, the family members may be apprehensive at the prospect of meeting again many of the same people who were present at the funeral. Just as in the case of the funeral, some planning should go into this important family and community event. Often the month's mind Mass will also be a parish Mass. This offers an opportunity for the wider community to share in the grief of the family. In the situation following a suicide, it will be important for a priest or pastoral worker to plan the liturgy with the same sensitivity as was noted in connection with the funeral.

For the family, relatives and friends, hearing the name of the deceased being mentioned at the month's mind brings back the memories and the tears. Following the suicide of a young person, there may be a large gathering of peers who will again find it strange that one of their age group should already be dead. The young associate death with older people: often it will be the passing of a grandparent that first brings them into close contact with death. Now they have to face again the fact that it is one of their own age who is gone.

Even though it will bring painful memories to the surface, coming together one month after the death can be a healing experience for the bereaved. Though it is very early days yet, the family have got this far and will meet again to affirm each other as well as to remember the deceased. This gathering around each other in support and love is a powerful force for good and can lead to the beginning of recovery. For a person of faith, the Mass assures them again that the deceased one is safe in the company of God. For a person without belief in the afterlife, a coming together soon after a death can also have a strong impact and contribute to healing.

In the weeks and months after a suicide, there are people so deeply affected by what has happened that they keep social contact outside of their home to a minimum. The thought of going out is almost unthinkable. For some, it is painful to face the world of ordinary life. The fear of meeting people not seen since the suicide is dreaded. This is not a criticism nor is there any suggestion that something is wrong. It is a fact that the pastoral worker can keep in mind. There may be some gentle and non-threatening opportunities that may be suggested, though always without pressure.

For some religious people, not being able to face going to church is painful. This is not a case of anger with God so much as an inability to re-enter into a community that once meant so much and gave so much comfort and support. Now in the aftermath of the suicide, what was once a place of comfort has become a place associated with unhappy memories. The pastoral worker may find a way of helping such a person re-establish contact with the church community. The reconnecting with the community of believers can, in time, become a source of comfort and the place where a fleeting experience of peace may be found. However, it is good to keep in mind that people heal very slowly and at different rates.

Visiting the Grave

Local customs vary with regard to remembering the dead. Pastoral carers will be aware of how sensitive the issue of visiting the grave of the loved one can be. It is by listening to what is being said that the various opinions about visiting the grave can be gained. There is no one 'right' way to deal with this matter of visiting. Some will want to spend a lot of time at the last resting place of the loved one. Others just can't bring themselves to go there as it hurts too much. There have been instances where a person may spend long periods of time at the grave, sometimes on their own. Other family members may become concerned about the amount of time this person is spending in the cemetery. They may just want to be close to the resting place of the loved one and this must be respected.

Family members may welcome help in addressing their concerns about time spent at the grave. A pastoral carer may be able to help in a gentle manner by expressing understanding and offering an opportunity to listen to the feelings of this person. If this does not meet with a positive response, the pastoral carer can still remain involved by keeping up contact and enquiring how the person is feeling.

Marking the Grave
While some family members may keep away from the cemetery in the early days and weeks, choosing a headstone to mark the grave will arise if the burial took place in a new grave. If the burial took place in a family grave, the inscription to be added to the headstone will arise. Some families will find a certain peace in this as it gives a sense that something is being done for the one who has died. This can also give a chance to express in some permanent way the strength of feelings for the loved one and what their loss means. Of course, no headstone or memorial will ever capture the

enormity of the loss or even begin to fill the gap that is there every day and night.

Some families opt for a very simple headstone with few adornments. Others will want something striking that expresses their loss. A priest or minister may be asked to bless this headstone when it is put in place. While this is not a regular occurrence, if the opportunity arises it can be greatly appreciated by the family. Over the years I have come to see how much this means to a family after any bereavement. Following a death by suicide, I wonder if the family appreciate it so much because it lays to rest any suspicion that somehow a person who dies by suicide is not really 'wanted' in a Catholic cemetery. Most parishes have an annual blessing of graves and again this can be a time of remembrance and showing that the loved one is not forgotten.

Memoriam Cards

Even before the funeral takes place, samples of memoriam cards may arrive in the post. A memoriam card is another way of remembering. These cards can have a photograph of the deceased with some message of love and remembrance. Some include words of Scripture or a prayer. Following the suicide of a young person, the card may bear emblems of a football team or some other imagery that meant a lot to the deceased. Some families will put a picture of the one who died on the front of the card. Words of a song or poem are sometimes included. There is something healthy in being able after a suicide to place the photo of the deceased on the front of the memoriam card. This does not disguise in any way the tragedy that their death was for everyone but it is a way of honouring their memory. A prayer is sometimes also included on the card as a sign of belief in the afterlife.

In this matter, real sensitivity is needed by the pastoral carer. I never comment one way or another on the design and content of such cards. I have a number of memoriam cards in the prayer book I use daily. They keep alive memories of the one who died and whose family are working through a loss that will never fully heal.

Birthdays and Anniversaries

Some people love celebrating birthdays, wedding anniversaries and other significant events. The arrival of the deceased loved one's birthday, even in families who are not 'into' birthday parties, brings back with intensity the memory of someone who is no longer present and the tangle of emotions that accompany the loss. As their birthday dawns, the memories of their birth and early years will be remembered by parents, and possibly grandparents and other family members. The birthday that once brought excitement and joy in the family is now a time of pondering what might have been. The 'why' and 'what if' questions surface again with renewed intensity. Whether there is belief in the afterlife or not, remembering a birthday of one who has died is tough for people looking at a bleak time ahead. Just as the one who died was special and unique, so the way of remembering and grieving is also special and deeply personal. However, the chasm left by the suicide cannot be filled and no attempt should be made to do so. Any offer of support from the pastoral worker at this time will make a great difference.

The first wedding anniversary since the suicide of a partner can also be a time of great sorrow. The remaining partner of the marriage faces a lonely time of remembering. A man who lost his wife told me that he would never recover from his loss. The anniversaries, birthdays and other special occasions for his family were nothing short of a nightmare.

The first anniversary of the death is especially difficult. Some want little or nothing done to mark the day; others will mark it publicly by way of a religious remembrance. This day will always be remembered as the day their world changed irrevocably. It can mean a great deal for the family if a priest or pastoral carer, who was there at the time of the suicide, can visit or make some contact at this point. This may not be easy but it can mean more to the family than it is possible to describe.

For some, the first anniversary can be a time to start forgiving the one who died by suicide. It may be difficult to admit but family members and friends may still need to come to peace with what happened. Where such is the case, the first anniversary, while being a moment of great sorrow, can also be an important opportunity to let the past slip gently away and begin to hope for a new future. This is not easy for people who are only beginning to come to terms with their loss; it demands great courage and love.

Civic society and religious communities remember their dead in the month of November. There are Remembrance Day ceremonies to honour those who died in two world wars. Catholic Churches around the world are packed for the celebration of the Feast of All Souls commemorating all the dead. On that night in Holy Cross Church, Belfast, the names of all who had been buried since 2 November the previous year are read out. When the name is announced each family carries forward a candle in remembrance of the loved one. Numerous people have spoken to me of what the collective presence of so many grieving people gave them by way of consolation. A lovely moment is when at the end of the ceremony each of the families is called forward to take home a simple wooden cross as a token of solidarity in suffering.

For many people, the first Christmas after a death by suicide is almost unbearable as the absence of the loved one cannot but speak loudly of pain and loss. Like all other such times, families will deal with the first Christmas and each subsequent one in their own way.

Each family and community of people has their own way of coping in the years following their loss. Pastoral carers have one great gift still to give in these months and years: their presence and their time. As a priest, I know that people can be immensely appreciative of a visit for no other purpose than to see how the family members are doing. The family knows, as do pastoral carers, that there is no instant solution to pain and the sense of loss. But sometimes a simple thing can make a difference. I was once brought to see a small tree in a back garden planted in memory of the one who died by suicide. This living tree is one way of remembering the one who died. Other families may choose a stone with verses that can be placed somewhere in the house or garden to mark not the loss but the presence of the loved one. A beautiful painting of the deceased may be too much for some people, but I know a family who draw great consolation from such a reminder. We are all different.

A Way Forward

The milestones mentioned here are important. But life is never as predictable as this. For no apparent reason, the loved one's presence can seem almost tangible at moments that have no obvious connection. The tears may come and the feeling of loss is once again as intense as it was on the day of the death. The person should be specially remembered at that moment because they are very close. Their presence is not an illusion. Their love for those left behind did not end the day they died. They still want to carry forward the relationship and they don't want to be excluded. Their 'nickname' can be used as readily now as ever. In the world of the spirit there is only a tissue-thin veil between those who are here and those who are gone to God.

Maybe the challenge is to learn how to love the one who died in a new way. The truth cannot be denied that the person is deceased and is not coming back, but all the ties of friendship do not unravel with death. The love that once bound people together does survive death and can be developed in the hope of eventual reunion. For a believer in eternal life this is a most wonderful and encouraging road to a new and warm relationship with the one who died.

If we could begin to develop this new love relationship with the one who has died, what a difference it would make to anyone carrying the pain of loss. The one who died was buried or cremated but the deep truth is that besides carrying their coffin, we can carry them in our hearts. And where closer can a person be to us than in our hearts?

Chapter 8

Suicide Support Groups

In April 2003, around the time I first came into contact with suicide in Belfast, it was clear that very little was in place locally to help the family and community to cope. Within months, as suicide followed suicide, it was obvious that more was needed than nine-to-five, Monday-to-Friday office hours. Suicides can happen on Bank Holiday weekends, in the early hours of Sunday morning or Christmas and New Year. In fact, times when families and friends gather to celebrate can plunge some people into crisis. The contrast between their loneliness and the merriment around them can bring on suicidal thoughts. When a crisis occurs at weekends, there is the added issue that hospitals tend to be at their busiest. I can recall sitting for hours during the night with a young person and their friends, waiting to see a doctor. Often, after waiting for hours, the young person would get fed up and simply stand up and leave. Hospitals were doing their best to deal with such a variety of calls. But such explanations are of little help to a family when a daughter or son is in crisis.

An added complication in those early days of my experiences with suicide was that some in danger of ending their own lives had consumed alcohol or taken drugs. After waiting many hours for medical attention, it was tough to hear in the early hours of the morning that the best that could be recommended was to let the person sleep and keep a careful eye on them. One of the most encouraging aspects that I observed was the loyalty and support offered by friends and companions of the person in crisis. There was never a need for me to go searching for people to come to the hospital or to help care for the one in crisis. This has remained with me as a sign of hope, knowing that there is a generosity of spirit in people, especially the young, that is not always acknowledged.

This chapter presents some background on groups that offer support and a listening ear to anyone needing to be heard by another human being. It also looks at how some statutory groups as well as voluntary ones can be resources both for anybody needing help and for the pastoral carer. While the national help networks do much needed work, a local community creating its own particular way of supporting bereaved people is recommended. Besides caring and supporting in the aftermath of a suicide, a local suicide group can also help promote suicide prevention within the framework of its own local community. The combined effectiveness of people united shoulder to shoulder in the face of suicide is very powerful.

Bereaved People Standing Shoulder to Shoulder
Sometimes individuals, whom we might call 'average people', after being so deeply wounded by the suicide of a loved one, can muster up the immense courage to turn their pain into action to save others from going down the same path. These people, heartbroken by the suicide in their own family, begin to ask what can be done and how they can help. I have witnessed this myself, often against my expectations, and it has been an honour to walk alongside them and help in any way I could.

These people who come forward like this are realistic. They know there is no easy solution to the growing incidence of suicide in our midst; they know they don't have a life-belt that can be thrown in a crisis to prevent another suicide; but they put themselves forward and offer the hope and support that might make the difference. When I became involved with a suicide prevention group in 2003, I could not have predicted how influential and important suicide support groups would become.

I would like to give a brief description of the genesis of one such group, PIPS, *www.pipsproject.com* and what can be achieved. The Public Initiative for the Prevention of Suicide and Self-harm takes its name from a seventeen-year-old, known as Pip to his friends, who died by suicide in the grounds of Holy Cross Monastery in Belfast on 23 April 2003.

Shock, devastation and brokenness were tangible in the hours and days following Pip's death. After the heartbreak of the funeral and saying goodbye to Pip, fear about what was happening among us surfaced. Care to prevent this coming to any other family was foremost in people's minds. This was new territory for us and we went from one reaction to another.

Fear gave way to anger when so little help was forthcoming from government departments that would assist a devastated community work through what had happened to Pip. It was difficult to know where to begin in seeking help from statutory services. Looking back now, it is clear that health boards and other services were not sufficiently engaged with local communities to respond to suicide. In those days government agencies promised help once an assessment of need was made. What the local community needed was help delivered more quickly and effectively. Long-term planning must take place, but immediate help is essential in the face of a terrifying crisis. I was afraid that the occurrence of suicide could spiral out of control. Sheer hard work and straight talking within the community affected brought a ray of hope. A solid community base began to challenge government and local services. This led to a slow but eventually productive partnership. It is in this dialogue and co-operation that a group can come to be.

Pip's father and a few other people took up the challenge of putting something in place to help those bereaved by suicide. They wanted also to prevent others dying in the same way. Based in the heart of their community, it was not long before they began to receive offers of help and support. They had no offices at this stage; they were simply people who made themselves available to answer a call from anyone of any age or religion that needed help when suicide seemed their only option. Bit by bit, these people became a focal point. My role as a pastoral worker in those early days was to support these small steps. Family support and suicide prevention from the beginning never belong to any one religious or political outlook. In the deeply divided community existing in Belfast this was remarkable.

Tragic deaths within a community due to suicide arise. This can happen anywhere and in some places there may be no group available locally to offer support. The immediate response is, of course, to be with the families in their time of loss. There is so much to be done immediately. In the longer term, a pastoral worker should not hesitate to seek out any of the support groups already in place. Asking advice or help from such groups will be met with a positive response. People bereaved by suicide, who are engaged in suicide prevention and support, have a fellow-feeling for those who approach them for help. In France, where I now live and minister, suicides are numerous. A training day for people in recognising danger signs relating to suicide and how to deal with them is being delivered in Paris by PIPS from Belfast. No pastoral worker need hesitate in seeking to create in their area the creation of a support group.

PIPS is built from the ground up and continues to grow and expand. It is built on rock. The foundations are preserving life, walking with the broken-hearted after a suicide and training people throughout the community to be aware of possible signs of suicide. It now offers advice and support in setting up similar groups wherever the need is expressed. Government task forces on suicide policy and plans have looked to PIPS for suggestions and evaluation of what is proposed.

The only true 'experts' that I know in the field of suicide are brave people who battle through their own loss by giving hope to others in crisis. Of course, there are great doctors, researchers and institutes of various sorts trying to understand and combat suicide. But when people bereaved by suicide speak, there is compassion born out of their own pain.

The other great power evident in suicide groups is that they speak with the authority of experience. When they speak of more help and better services being needed, government and local health authorities listen because these people do not give up and don't go away. In any health budget there are so many groups rightly calling for funding. Until comparatively recently, the threat of suicide was not taken seriously in many communities. It has been heartbreaking for me to go to so many places and listen to story after story of death by suicide. These stories vary from 'out of the blue' without any warning signs being picked up, to the broken spirit of the person giving great concern for their safety. In the allocation of funds, suicide support groups rightly call for a rethink of how governments approach the whole area of suicide.

Support Services

As far back as 1953 a young vicar in London called Chad Varah started what we know today as the **Samaritans**. They have over 202 branches in the UK and Ireland. Reverend Varah set up his emergency phone counselling service out of his own pastoral experience in dealing with suicidal people. Suicide would remain a criminal offence in the UK until 1961, so suicidal people were very reluctant to seek help. The first call was made to the Samaritans on 2 November 1953, the date now regarded as the birthday of the Samaritans. As we saw in the previous chapter this date has special significance. The Samaritans website is *www.samaritans.org*

Aware is an Irish voluntary organisation formed in 1985 to provide support to those whose lives are directly affected by depression. Aware estimates that one in ten people in Ireland suffers from depression and that one in three people will be affected, directly or indirectly, by it in their lifetime. Because many people hide their depression they don't seek the help they urgently need. Aware works to bring support to sufferers of depression and their families. They also seek to dispel the myths and misunderstandings of this devastating illness. Aware support groups offer an opportunity to talk openly about depression and its impact. Their helpline operates 365 days a year. Their website is *www.aware.ie*

Console is a group that was born in 2002 from the courage of one person who had lost a loved one through suicide. Console has grown into an effective and wonderful group operating throughout the Republic of Ireland. In being associated with Console for many years, I have come to appreciate their dedication to those bereaved by suicide and determination to prevent further loss of life. The website is *www.console.ie*

Teenline was started in Dublin by a mother whose sixteen-year-old son had taken his life by suicide on 6 April 2003. After talking to her son's friends she courageously set up this group to raise awareness of suicide. In July 2006, a freephone helpline was opened up. Volunteers that month answered 110 calls; in April 2009 they answered 1,185 calls dealing not only with suicide prevention, but with young people who were feeling anxious, depressed or worried.

There are so many groups I have met in different places that have come into existence in response to a local death by suicide, such as PIPS mentioned earlier. People are most powerful when their loss is turned into effective action on behalf of others. These groups mentioned above make a magnificent contribution in helping those in distress and do all they can to save lives. A full listing would be impossible, but pastoral carers should check the internet to find out what is available in their area. Just having a directory listing the groups ready to assist at short notice can prove to be a real contribution to care for people who need help urgently.

Raising Awareness

It is impossible to overstate the value of suicide support groups. When no hope exists and there seems to be no future, it is crucial that a listening person, a phone line or some trusted form of contact be known and available to the suffering person or someone close to them. It is not easy to decide to ask for help at any age. For many people there is still a sense of failure in admitting that they cannot go on. By raising awareness of the 'normality' of seeking help when things go wrong, a crisis may be averted.

There is no doubt in my mind that there are people alive today because of the suicide awareness training that has been delivered to many individuals and groups. These groups provide simple but effective training to people of all ages and abilities. A pastoral carer, not dealing directly with suicide prevention or support, may at some stage be called upon to point someone in the direction of such help and support. The more that is known of groups in the area in which a person lives, the more ready the response when an emergency arises.

Suicide support groups provide empowerment for key people – parents, teachers, nurses, general practitioners, police, youth leaders, clergy, fire service – and others to watch out for people who may be at risk. The effectiveness of this approach came home to me just before Christmas 2006 when I received a phone call from a mother at about 8.00 a.m. Her son, travelling to work on the upper deck of a bus, told her he had seen a young man walking through the church grounds with a travel bag in his hand. He said something could be the matter as he thought it did not look 'right'. Sure enough, when I got to the monastery garden there was a young man, whom I knew, who was in a very distressed state and was preparing to end his life. Sitting with him for a chat, he calmed down and handed over the bag. In it there was a rope and a bottle of vodka. Once safely back home with his family, the immediate crisis had passed. The phone call from a man on a bus to his mother ensured that another family did not have a funeral that Christmas. That young man going to work had saved a life because he was aware of the danger signs of suicide.

People in suicide support groups stand in solidarity with the bereaved in the immediate aftermath of a suicide. Their support and healing work is not limited to those few frantic days leading up to the funeral. It is just as essential when things have quietened down and the house is no longer full and buzzing. There are many long and lonely days, and even worse nights, when the emptiness of loss seems almost unbearable. A visit from volunteers of a suicide group assures the broken-hearted that they are not alone and need never be. Contact from such support groups also tells the family that it is possible to survive and that hope is not ridiculous.

It is difficult to appreciate how helpful pastoral carers are in the outreach to families. Just being available when needed is so appreciated. There are no sure and certain ways of knowing how to be of most support and assistance other than by never forgetting that pastoral helpers and clergy are there for the sake of the bereaved. There may seem to be little that can be done, but to be there counts a great deal.

A number of families have told me how much they appreciated knowing that there was someone they could contact when the going got really tough. If the pastoral carer has experienced loss, this can be of solid help as they recall their own journey through grief and desolation. Clergy can be a comfort for the family by providing a line of continuity from discovery of the suicide through the funeral into the aftermath.

If I have learned anything from walking with families in these impossibly difficult times it is that making assumptions about what should be done and what is needed can lead to unintentional hurt and misunderstanding. Every family is different. Some families warmly welcome the pastoral carer or clergy while others are more reserved. I have seen some families who were not keen on having visits or even contact with support groups at the time of the suicide. In time, some of these come around to not just acceptance of support but become involved themselves. Others may wish to deal with their loss and grief without any such involvement. If pastoral care was for the sake of the carer, then there could be disappointment or a feeling of rejection. But all such reaching out is for the sake of those who have lost a loved one and is never about the pastoral carer.

Offering a Way Forward

As has already been mentioned, it can be difficult for the bereaved to re-enter the world of social activity outside the home following a death by suicide. A first step for some is to accept an invitation to an event where the focus is loss by suicide. I know one suicide support group that has gathered families and friends every Advent to simply remember their loved one as Christmas approaches. There are candles, magnificent music, singing, dance and a few prayers. It is very poignant when, in the silence of the huge group assembled, each person holds a candle for the one who is no longer with them. Following this, the Christmas lights are switched on. It has been a great honour for me to be associated with this event each year. I have met people in so many different places who mention how much this event has done for them. The reason for this might be the positive affirmation they receive that they are not alone.

A huge amount of work goes into the preparation of this event during the whole year. The care with which every aspect of the celebration is prepared shows the families how much they are appreciated. On the day itself, pastoral workers and clergy need have no designated role other than just being there. After the event, it has been my experience that conversation begins about the one who has died and how much the loss means. To be present and listening is all that is asked. To attempt any more is to miss what is most important.

Another group, in Belfast, lights its Christmas tree outdoors with people from both sides of an otherwise divided community present. These people, who traditionally live such separate lives, stand together in remembrance and prayer for the one who is gone. The solidarity in loss and in hope far outweighs religious or political differences. If ever the tragedy of suicide has given birth to a positive outcome, it is in this coming together of a divided community. In the telling of their stories, there is the realisation that the tears are the same and the challenges no different. Clergy of different denominations standing together in such a context show that the grief and loss far surpasses any political or religious differences. Suicide support workers will witness to the same supremacy of compassion over all else.

There is a great need for celebrations of life and light, and not just at Christmas. One group each year arranges a Mass of Hope to remember with love and affection those who have died by suicide. Remembering in silence, while holding a light for a deceased one, is powerful. While nothing can replace the one who has gone, such moments give a glimpse into eternity where the loved one now resides. For maybe just a split second, there is contact and the pain eases, even if just a little.

In suicide support groups, those who have not been personally bereaved are conscious of being in the presence of very special people. These people have walked in places where I have not been and are determined to help prevent further loss by suicide.

People bereaved by suicide are so respectful of how delicate and fragile people are in the aftermath of a suicide. Maybe as they step over the threshold into the home of a bereaved family, they whisper a prayer for guidance. They know from experience that the hand they are going to shake, the cheek they may kiss or the person they may hug is like fine china. They are fragile not because they are weak people but because they are coming out of an experience beyond anything that a human being ever imagined would happen to them. This is holy ground, in my view, because it is the Calvary of the twenty-first century. The dawn of resurrection looks so distant. This is the sacred place that the suicide support group enters and faces with bravery.

As people from suicide groups engage with others, they are simply standing beside the bereaved person and doing no more than being present in this moment of loss. In religious terms, they are 'a sacrament of presence' giving nourishment to hungry people. They may say very little in words but their action of being there and caring speaks volumes. Such volunteers are so honest that they do not offer easy answers. They can't because they don't have them. This is a ministry of 'like to like' and it is the power and effectiveness of suicide support groups.

In all of this, the pastoral carer is there to accompany others who are bearing the pain of loss. In other areas of helping within the community, pastoral workers often have a lead role. In the walk of life with families after a suicide this may not be the case. The place is beside the person. Especially when the pastoral carer carries the loss of a loved one by suicide in their heart, they know that just to be there is enough.

Prevention

Some suicide support groups have been effective in speaking to school groups, especially at secondary level. In the aftermath of a suicide in a school, great support and help is needed. But even without the tragedy of a loss of life, the young people are aware of suicide. Many of them will have suicidal thoughts, even if only of a transitory nature. Some may be depressed and not see much hope in their future. A suicide support group can be a beacon of light showing that there is a way out other than ending one's life. Without hope, there is no future. A reason to live is essential for going forward. The agreement of schools and parents to have the issue of suicide raised shows their commitment to mental health issues that are often not easily spoken about. There is credibility about suicide support groups communicating with young people because of their own experience of loss and pain.

Some support groups, in their battle to prevent suicides in the future, highlight the need for more beds being provided when emergencies arise. They also offer various therapies to help people deal with stress and depression. Clear and helpful lines of communication are being established with the medical profession and health care providers.

When I first became aware of the reality of suicide, I was often at a loss to know what to do when a crisis developed outside of doctors' or health service hours. One day, a highly qualified nurse phoned me to say that she was aware of the alarming increase in suicides in the area surrounding where I lived. Her offer of help was remarkably simple but hugely important: she gave me her mobile phone number and told me I could call 24/7. She will never know how much her call meant to me or how grateful people were when I was able to act on her suggestion. This is just one example of how a generous gesture can have a great effect. Pastoral carers may sometimes underestimate how their own gifts and skills can be of enormous help to people battling through difficult times.

Part of the mission of existing support groups is to help others starting out. In cases where a suicide occurs in an area where there is no support group, if even a few people concerned about the lack of such a group participate in a training day, the seed is sown for a new group to emerge. Health boards can also be of help in pointing people in the right direction.

As a priest, I would suggest that every parish or cluster of parishes should have the capacity to become a focal point for initiating a suicide support group. This does not make it a religious group only for believers. As the main faiths come together on the issue of suicide and work together to create awareness of the need of suicide support, a powerful message is being given. A strong 'pro-life' message and a powerful witness to the sanctity of every human life from conception until God calls a person home can be given in this way.

People who have been bereaved by the suicide of colleagues or friends can take the step of becoming involved in suicide prevention and support groups. The availability of training courses is increasing. This first step can lead to support groups becoming an accepted part of every community's care for those in need of a helping hand over a temporary obstacle in their lives. This is surely much better than to have suicides continue to increase.

The frequency of road safety publicity, even with some disturbing and graphic imagery, is to be welcomed once lives are being saved. Suicide prevention groups, without needing to employ graphic images, give a powerful message through the witness of their members. These volunteers refuse to give up on the hope of preventing other families from ever knowing the same pain of loss that is theirs.

Chapter 9

Specific Needs
of the Pastoral Worker

In every generation there are people with an unflinching love for others. They sacrifice their ambitions for the sake of other people. A person may give all they have over many years to care for a parent or relative. Often, there is no financial gain; there can even be a lack of gratitude shown by those helped. The overwhelming majority of these people get no public recognition nor do they seek it. They are hidden heroes.

It has been my good fortune to meet many such people over my lifetime. Attending an annual awards ceremony in Dublin to salute heroic people, I have been impressed by how self-effacing these people are. Almost all would prefer not to receive such public recognition. Some of the recipients have been young children who acted quickly to avert a tragedy at home. Others, from the emergency services, put the safety of another person ahead of their own safety.

There are fantastic people who do not belong to any helping organisation but do great work for anyone in need. A good and caring neighbour can be of immense value to a person suffering intensely in body or spirit. Being a good neighbour is immensely valuable, especially as isolation and loneliness are features of contemporary living.

So far, the pastoral carer has been seen from the perspective of someone whose activity brings them into contact with needy people in a defined and organised way. Those reaching out can be a teacher, psychologist, social worker, medical personnel, police, youth worker, counsellor, member of clergy or church organisation, etc. Suicide awareness and prevention groups bring together enthusiastic people who give generously of their talents and time in reaching out to others in need.

Dealing with people is both a privilege and a challenge. It is a privilege because it allows entry into the world of another person and sharing in the most precious and sacred aspects of their life. For a believer, this is captured in seeing this person as a precious child of God. For those without a religious belief it is sharing in the solidarity of humanity on this earth trying to live a dignified and fully human life. For all, it is a selfless act of giving, neither counting the cost nor seeking any reward or recognition.

We can only imagine how much poorer our world would be without people who care for others. It seems that such generous people give to others with ease.

But there *is* a cost for the one who is caring and giving. Sometimes such people are the last to realise the toll this is taking on them. Because the demands can be huge, clear boundaries for their engagement are essential if fatigue and ultimately breakdown are to be avoided. In a suicide support group, carers need to be particularly aware of these pitfalls because of the nature of the engagement involved. Suicide is not a theoretical issue that can be kept at a distance. Volunteers in support groups and pastoral workers who offer great availability need to take care of their own mental and physical health. The question of who cares for the carers is one that needs constant attention.

This final chapter will deal primarily with the person who does the caring. If the carer's inner world runs into difficulties, then the help and support they give to others will be affected. Helpers need to keep hope alive in their own hearts if they are to give it to others. No one can give what they have not got themselves. This chapter will stress the importance of pastoral workers looking after their own health and well-being. It will suggest ways to avoid burn-out, fatigue and crippling fear. Pastoral carers need to assess their present situation in the light of how they are dealing with their past and plan their future. Supervision regularly entered into by the pastoral carer will keep these under review. The value of the pastoral worker will be highlighted, with their caring being seen more as a vocation than a job.

In professional and paid counselling and other therapeutic engagements, protocols and supervision are put in place. This is crucial. In some pastoral groups it can be very easy for safeguards against fatigue and breakdown to be either absent or far down on the list of priorities. Some groups do pay attention to this and provide structured opportunities for carers to regularly review, renew and plan for their future engagement to fulfil the stated mission of the support group.

There is a danger in working without boundaries. Out of a sense of generosity, volunteers may feel they must respond to every need. It is extremely difficult in the area of suicide prevention to avoid this. There is often a very short time span in which to act when the emergency arises. To lose that spontaneous generosity in responding would be tragic. The intention here is not to become bound by hours of business or selectivity regarding response to emergencies. It has everything to do with the pastoral carer surviving in this most demanding of activities. Some basic ways in which the individual carer can be personally helped will be suggested. These can be supplemented and enriched by other approaches that address the particular circumstances of the carer.

Supervision

Over twenty years ago, while studying pastoral ministry at the University of San Francisco, USA, I trained in counselling of primary school children. That was when I first came across a discipline that was new to me, namely, 'Supervision'. A condition of training, required by the university, was that I accept being in weekly supervision. Three hours communal supervision with other trainee counsellors and one hour on an individual basis were required if I was to qualify.

As a priest of some sixteen years' experience at that time, I was mildly surprised that I was being asked to do this. But it turned out to be a great learning experience. Since then I have always asked myself who can monitor not only what I do but how I am while doing it. In the light of revelations of abuse by members of religious congregations and clergy, questions must be raised about the absence of supervision and the loss of direction of these groups. Supervision creates a safeguard for all concerned.

In many helping organisations there are policies on various aspects – patients' charters in hospitals, child protection in schools and youth clubs – that are regularly updated. In some instances, it is a legal requirement to have protocols in place. In the area of pastoral caring and outreach, especially where volunteers are concerned, I believe there should be a written policy on how each group will care for their people both as individuals and in their work for the organisation.

It is possible to give assent to the critical importance of such a way of operating in theory, but not believe that it really applies to me as a member. Under supervision, a pastoral carer cannot avoid becoming aware of their own strengths, weaknesses and needs. If as a priest or pastoral carer I adopt, even subconsciously, a 'messiah' or 'superman' mentality, then I am in danger of believing I must keep going no matter what the personal cost. Delusion can easily set in. Even though I may not articulate it, I may believe that I an indispensable.

Some people reach a stage where they are afraid to stop their activity because it can be too painful to look at what is emerging and happening in their own life. An individual or a group can continue doing what they have always done, perhaps more out of habit than of conviction. This is both serious and sad.

There are many examples of admirable people who didn't spare themselves. A great missionary like Blessed Teresa of Calcutta can be put forward as an exemplar. Other examples of utter generosity in giving to others may come to mind. Carers may begin to feel guilty if they are not in that same mould. It is tempting to take on a hero to imitate. Trying to identify as closely as possible with such a person is not necessarily a good thing. What pastoral carers do for suicide support and prevention is not to fulfil personal aspirations but to support others and to save lives.

Supervision is best seen as a gift to carers rather than an imposition. This enables them to recover their inner health and well-being and continue to do their work more effectively. Pastoral supervision is a recognised discipline and one that is already well-established in helping professions. It is my hope that pastoral supervision and education will become much better known in the future.

Pastoral supervision is needed in suicide prevention groups both for the sake of the volunteer and for their outreach to those in distress. In Chapter 2, the carer's need of advice and direction was mentioned when confidentiality arises in reporting a threatened suicide. Supervisors are invaluable support people in this area also and can help volunteers know they are not alone.

The dedication and generosity of people in suicide prevention groups may leave them negligent in looking after themselves. Their priority is to reach out to others in need and pain. At the risk of being sexist and also wrong, it seems to me that men are not as ready to share their feelings and anxieties as women. Still, it is important for male and female pastoral carers to have a planned and regular structure of supervision whereby the person, and not only the activity, is cared for and strengthened. Through supervision it is easier to become aware of the personal help that is needed and where it can be found.

Personal deterioration can creep up on a person without their being aware of what is developing. Then a point is reached where 'burnout', 'compassion fatigue' and such like take over. With structured supervision this is less likely to happen. Warning bells will be heard earlier. The support group that invests in its members will be handsomely rewarded with the well-being of their staff and in the quality of the work done.

When the going is really tough, the last thing we may want to do is to take a break from what is challenging us. Yet, a short break can unblock whatever was preventing progress. In supervision we might be told that until we change, the situation will not change or improve. It can be a tough message to receive but at a deep level I know it is true.

The truth is that there is no limit to what can and should be done to deal with suicide, self-harm and to offer family support after such a death. Physically, emotionally, psychologically and spiritually, the carer can grow in all of these areas because of their engagement. Equally, however, one person cannot achieve everything. Such engagement, without reflection, can bring a person into poor health.

Supervision shows that the mind must remain open if the unique truth of each new situation is to be appreciated. If the point is reached where the carer is slipping into the fallacy that they have done all this before, much of what is happening in the new situation will be missed. So also the heart must remain open so that new relationships may be made in each new situation. There is a danger that the carer may want to stop or reduce their involvement but guilt in the face of need stops them from admitting this. In supervision, this can be articulated and resolved without leaving the person carrying a sense of guilt.

The nearest religious model for supervision, even though different in some ways, is spiritual direction, where a person invites another to visit their mind, heart and will, not to judge but for the betterment of the person.

My own involvement in this area of suicide care would not have been possible without the support and overview offered by another person. This person gave generously of his time in a busy family and professional life to ensure that I had a listening person never far away. He could see how deeply affected I was by what I saw of suicide deaths and their aftermath. He could mirror back to me what was happening to my spirit and well-being. He helped keep me sane and mentally healthy in some very difficult and trying circumstances. Another great support was a good doctor and attentive nurse who understood my circumstances and who kept a watch for any warning signs of ill health, either physical or mental.

The other wonderful area of support and care that I have found are suicide support groups such as PIPS and Console. These groups not only look out for those at risk of suicide but those among them who are at risk of personal health deterioration.

Organisations have needs as well as individuals. The health of the organisation needs to be monitored as well lest the group loses its way and 'forgets' why it exists. Large numbers of religious congregations in the history of the Catholic Church have disappeared after a longer or shorter time in existence. Some had fulfilled the purpose for which they were founded while others got lost and no longer had a clear sense of direction.

Few suicide support groups are more than a decade old. Their effectiveness and continuing existence will depend on remaining focused on their purpose of giving the care their membership needs. The vitality of the group depends to a large extent on the health and well-being of the membership.

Pastoral Care as a Vocation

While all forms of pastoral care involve a generous spirit, the engagement in the area of suicide prevention or outreach is best described as being a vocation. It is a call that demands a lot of the carer and is much more than a defined function or precise activity in which one engages. While many professionals are engaged at various stages around a suicide, the volunteer's care does not arise from their profession but from their free choice to be present. This is not meant as a denigration of professionals who do such wonderful work in the area of suicide. But it is intended to underline that volunteers (either in pastoral teams or in bereavement groups) deserve structured care and support as outlined above. This is essential because of the often unstructured nature of their involvement.

Because people's needs are so great and the tragedy of suicide so emotionally draining, pastoral workers can have unrealistic expectations of themselves. It can also happen that in a support group some may have these unrealistic expectations of their fellow volunteers. The truth is that the work of suicide prevention and outreach to families is limitless. If a volunteer gets a reputation of being available when a crisis arises, it can mean that there is no 'off-duty time' as would occur in a paid profession. The ability to say 'no', as must happen, can cause real tension for the volunteer and within the support group.

When a person can give no more, this is not a sign of weakness. The danger is that it can be interpreted that way by others. There is a limit to the empathy that one can go on giving. This happens especially when a number of suicides or threats of suicide follow each other in quick succession. Feelings of fear, helplessness and personal inadequacy will all surface and leave a pastoral worker feeling lonely. Due to this, the carer begins to suffer, sleep patterns become unsettled and relationships deteriorate. Many pastoral carers and clergy, no matter what other activities they are engaged in, will seldom find anything so draining as sustained involvement in the area of suicide.

Pastoral carers will often be dealing with people from an increasingly secular society. Fundamental questions about life and its meaning will arise. Until recent times, religious faith was part of the very fabric of life. Now that is less frequently the case, more and more situations where there is no religious belief are being met. If the pastoral carer is a believer, lay or clerical, this non-religious faith context may cause some disquiet and unease. The deeper a person values their own faith and spirituality, the more they may struggle to engage with a world in which people have a different outlook.

A simple issue, for example, may be the absence of a belief in an afterlife. In the absence of an explicit religious faith, there still exists a strong and sustained desire to keep alive the memory of one so loved and missed, but sadly no longer around. To remember a loved one now dead is a beautiful refusal to allow the deceased to slip away into oblivion. All that was so valued in family and among friends until so recently retains value. Anyone who is remembered with love does not die forever.

Any vocation makes its own demands. The vocation to care for others in the realm of suicide must rank among the most challenging. Many pastoral workers come to do this out of their own experience of loss of someone through a suicide. They must be reminded that caring applies also to their own life and well-being.

Care within a Marriage and Priesthood

Caring may have another dimension that must not be neglected. A married person or someone in a relationship cannot take for granted that the other person accepts all the demands made on their time. If one party is not directly involved in the outreach of a suicide group it may help if they are invited to some activities of the group so that greater understanding can be gained.

Death by suicide is unlike any other loss. The aftermath can see relationships come under great strain, as no two people, no matter how close they arc in a relationship, will react in the same way. The fundamental importance of good communication is stressed in the preparation of couples for marriage. In the aftermath of a suicide, there cannot be enough emphasis placed on how crucial regular and honest communication will become for a couple where one partner is a pastoral worker. This partner may assume that the other knows what they are going through and how they feel. But so often I have heard it said that living with the pastoral carer has become next to impossible. There is no doubting the good work they are doing, but at what price to the marriage relationship? This is not the place to apportion blame but to highlight the need for vigilance so that misunderstanding and pain can be reduced.

Not all people are capable of opening up their inmost thoughts and emotions following the trauma of a death by suicide, even to one they love. It is no disgrace to admit their need of help. Any pastoral carer, especially clergy, may feel that they can cope and sort everything out by themselves. For many of us, that will not be so. At some stage, we will seek the listening ear of another who will allow us to express what is happening in our inner world. Where clergy are married, stress or trauma associated with their suicide ministry can affect their relationship.

It is sad that it is only when marriage breakdown or separation occurs that any help is sought or the truth revealed about how awful life had become. Just as the stigma surrounding suicide is diminishing, so the seeking of personal help is, thankfully, becoming an accepted part of life.

Clergy who are not married must deal with their issues also. Where there are other clergy living in the same house, it can be good to acquaint them with the challenges of engagement in the area of suicide. It is important for individual clergy not to be too proud to let another know when they are hurting.

Needing to be Needed

One of the dangers to watch out for in the area of pastoral care is the high level of satisfaction that comes with what is being done. It is possible to become addicted to working with people in trauma. Sometimes the 'buzz' associated with being needed and helping is missed when times are quiet. It is not that the pastoral worker wants anyone to be in danger. But when an emergency arises, the opportunity to respond is welcomed. The truth is that behind all that is happening and all that is being given so generously is one frail human being. Without going out of their way to attract people in need of help, the pastoral worker can be sucked into over-involvement to such a degree that illness and even breakdown is the outcome. If the needs of the carer are not addressed they will eventually get in the way of caring and then everyone loses. The bereaved may have the added burden of having a needy person around them when they feel unable to cope with their own lot. The carer may feel hurt or rejected if their needs are not taken into consideration.

The Value of the Pastoral Worker

Some carers, especially those who are religiously motivated, may think they should be the last to be cared for. It is not selfish to make caring for self a priority. It may be worthwhile for a believer to ponder how often Christ went away to a lonely place to pray and how he always spent time with his Father before making any decisions in his life and ministry.

For those without a religious faith, there is ample evidence of many places providing meditation, yoga and other activities designed to help the person to deal with stress.

Pastoral care of those bereaved by suicide is an intensely human activity that is deeply spiritual. A wounded person stands shoulder to shoulder with other wounded people and says it is going to be alright for you. True, it will never be the same again – he or she is not coming back – but together we can inch forward and find the beginning of healing.

To one whose pain is so bad that death would be a relief, we dare to invite them to step out of the shadow and into the light of hope. This is done not in a theory or in a lesson to be followed. It is done in letting the one hurting so much become aware that they are loved and that there is hope. If ever there was a need for a true companion, it is on the brink of despair. To show someone kindness and a belief in them can make all the difference.

A lot of pressure can be relieved for the pastoral worker by remembering the story of the lady who went into a shop and found God serving behind the counter. This was her chance and she asked for an impressive list of gifts – all good and wholesome, and not just for herself alone but for everyone on earth. The story goes that God smiled and told her that he didn't deal with full ripe fruits, but only with tiny seeds. Pastoral carers deal more with seeds than with fruits.

If this book sows a seed that offers life and hope to one person, it will have more than fulfilled its purpose.

Epilogue

Accompanying people affected by suicide has changed me more than I could ever have imagined. In putting these thoughts on paper, I have revisited in spirit and memory many people, places and events that have been part of my life over the past six years. If asked before starting to write, I would have said that these events were fixed firmly in my past. While I see some of these people from time to time and will never forget any of them, I thought I had moved on with my life. When I was transferred from Belfast to Paris at the end of September 2008, I would have said that I had drawn a line under the issue of suicide and its prevention. I have discovered this not to be the case and now know that it will never be.

This book, as indicated in the Introduction, makes no claim to being a full treatment of suicide or its prevention. It does not claim any authority in the area of suicide. It contains words from my heart inspired by people who opened their homes and hearts to me at a most awful time in their lives. Together we went through something of immense sorrow and pain that has created an unseen bond that will never be broken. Wherever they or I go, there is a bond that is forever connected with the death of their loved one. This connection is not quantifiable because it is a spiritual or, dare I suggest it, a mystical relationship.

Never have I found such depths of true spirituality to equal those in the circle of people bereaved by suicide or its threat to themselves or a loved one. People regarded as 'ordinary' rise to new levels and plumb depths that casual observation would, in all likelihood, regard as impossible. The wealth a parish or any community has in these people is beyond words and should be treasured and appreciated. Talk of suicide as a stigma must be banished once and for all. None of these people asked to be connected with suicide and its aftermath. But when it came knocking at their door, they proved to be worthy, often heroically, of their cross.

As I said at the start of this book, I came into this area of suicide not by choice but by circumstances. I would call it God's providence. This does not mean that I am more suited or gifted than others to be engaged in this area – I know for certain that such is not the case – but the ways of God are truly mysterious. The wonderful people I have met who have been affected by suicide never asked for this. The suicide will never be fully explained or maybe never totally accepted, but the loved one who died will eventually come home to the heart of the family in a new way. In time, by God's providence, this may come to be seen by those left to grieve. That is the secret of the unbreakable bond of love. Even suicide, with all that is dreaded about it, cannot break forever the links that bind us together.

Writing this book brought home to me what a debt of gratitude I owe to all who have trusted me and accepted me to walk with them since April 2003 in this most amazing world of suicide and its aftermath. This has changed me more than any of these people could ever know. This extraordinary time in my life came on the heels of the Holy Cross School blockade of 2001. The children, the families and the school community with whom I walked daily for three months changed me more profoundly than the formal studies and religious formation I had throughout my almost forty years as a Passionist priest. I didn't think that God would put me in any more situations at this late stage in my life that would continue to change me. But he did!

Meeting people bereaved by suicide or those tempted to end their life has helped me to see the beauty of life in its simplicity and not the complexity set out in many of the sermons I've preached over the years! Now what matters to me more than ever is friendship, love, and not hiding from my own vulnerability. It's about allowing others care for me as I try to care for them and never judging the why or wherefore of the mystery that we are to each other. People who have gone through the barrier of the familiar and the secure following a suicide have taught me about change and flexibility in my life. Their lives will never get back to what they were before the suicide. But they go on living and loving.

In the past, it took so little to upset me. Now I am ashamed of myself when I see what upset a suicide causes and yet people go on with life. While it is good to have a Rule of Life as a religious and a priest, it must never stand in the way of what is happening in real life.

Having lived in a religious community since I was eighteen years of age I thought I had a fair grasp of spiritual and religious issues. But to sit in houses, visit hospitals or morgues and to stand in graveyards or a crematorium has given me a new understanding of the spirituality of the Cross that comes straight from 'crucified' people. So many of these people are broken by the suicide and might be thought to have little left to offer. Once broken by the tragedy of suicide, so many of those most deeply affected communicate an emotional response in a truly magnificent way. They have been an inspiration for me in trying to communicate better an emotional response that is honest and genuine.

Throughout the chapters of this book I have dealt more with suicide among young people. There were more young deaths. But, I can recall so vividly the deaths by suicide of older people. When a parent of a family dies by suicide, the family is wounded deeply. Their pain is beyond words.

If the one who died is young, there is usually a gathering of big numbers of youth who may have relatively little experience of death. The reality of death may strike at a deep level for the first time. In an age that has seen so much violence and death on news programmes and in video games, it could be assumed that young people are well used to death. But my experience would indicate that the pain of loss is deep for the young who have lost one of their own generation. Indeed, when anybody of any age dies by suicide, there are so many people shocked, broken-hearted and traumatised.

Death and the supernatural are big issues for many people, the young included. Dealing with death by suicide takes great sensitivity on the part of parents, school, relatives and pastoral helpers, including clergy. It may be months or longer before the questions will surface about their friend who has died. Whatever form the questions take, it may be advisable not to answer these in a definite yes/no manner. There are often other issues behind these questions which are crucial to the health and sometimes to the survival of the young person asking. When they search for answers about life and an afterlife, there can often be more than a theoretical interest. Often what can be concealed in the question is something akin to a 'Russian Doll', the Matryoshka. You open one doll and find another one inside and so on until you get to the core where there is the final doll. Both in love and in grief, we may be guarded about our real questions and thoughts – the genuine object of our search – until we see how the outer layer is dealt with first. Only then do we dare go to the heart of the matter.

Sometimes the question as presented is all that is at stake and should be responded to at face value.

When more is at stake, it takes almost a 'sixth sense' to detect what more may be involved. This is where sharing and supervision mentioned earlier helps us to check out with experienced friends and colleagues how best to deal with these often complex situations. Also, by such sharing and the care under supervision, we are able to receive the support we need when faced with matters that can be of life or death significance. It is a huge responsibility but the rewards are great when a person in distress finds in one of us a person to whom a question can be put forward without fear of rejection.

One thing is certain from my experience in the area of suicide. There is a spiritual hunger and searching among people, especially the young, that is impressive and challenging for pastoral carers. Such an intense search I have also seen among those with no religious belief.

Involvement in the area of suicide will remain a part of my life. Every day I pray for those who have died by suicide. I also pray for those who mourn them, especially when the going is tough, that they may find someone who can show that there is hope. This can make the difference between life and death.

Acknowledgements

All whom I met on this journey in the shadow of death by suicide affected me more deeply than they can ever know. Just some of the suicides that occurred are mentioned but not one is forgotten or less important to me. That is why this book is dedicated to all who have allowed me walk with them. Each has a special place in my heart.

The generous assistance and advice from Console and PIPS about suicide prevention and support provided me with resources that were most helpful. The important events held by them brought me into contact with families bereaved by suicide. At these I learned the meaning of courage and the refusal to let hope die.

In the aftermath of every suicide, the courtesy and consideration shown by ambulance service, police, doctors, nurses, relatives, neighbours and so many other professional and voluntary services made me feel less alone.

How suicide is reported in media is important. Practically all whom I met in the course of engagement with suicide adhered to principles of respect and discretion in their reporting. This was appreciated by bereaved families. Various media outlets gave me an opportunity to lift part of the veil surrounding the issue of suicide.

This book is seeing the light of day because Donna Doherty of Veritas Publications believed in a need for it and my ability to write it. The support she has shown to me throughout was most helpful. Maura Hyland, Managing Director of Veritas, and other staff were constantly available to advise.

Michael Carroll, a friend for many years, made available to me material on supervision being prepared for publication that offered guidance in writing that section of the book.

Tom Heneghan, Religion Editor for Reuters, read the manuscript in its various drafts and offered advice that helped me shape and refine the book.

Finally, the parishioners of St Joseph's Parish, Paris, and my Passionist colleague here, Father Francis Finnigan, created a calm and supportive setting in which to write.

To all my sincere and profound gratitude.